THE
STRAIGHT FURROW
BY
FRED DIXON

SOME MEMOIRS OF
A SURREY VILLAGE SCHOOLMASTER
1936–1961

Newark Priory.

SEND & RIPLEY HISTORY SOCIETY

1. Fred Dixon

Foreword

Fred Dixon was born in 1896 in Westcott, near Dorking, the son of a grocer. His family came to Send in 1908 when his father was appointed manager of the Surrey Trading Company's shop, now Send Post Office. He attended Send Church of England School for two years.

After serving in the army throughout the First World War he trained to become a teacher. He held teaching posts in Addlestone, West Byfleet and Woking before his appointment as headmaster of Ripley Church School. Here he stayed for 25 years until his retirement in 1961.

The school was later closed following the opening of the new school at Georgelands. In 1981 the buildings where he taught were demolished to make way for the new terraced houses named Church Row.

Fred Dixon's story, written several years after he retired, gives a vivid impression of the educational system in village schools during a period of painful evolution. Much of his account already has the sepia quality of a distant era; yet it is within the living memory of many who attended the school. Whilst universal education was by then long established in Britain, the level of basic facilities in many schools left much to be desired. Ripley was typical in this respect. The standards which Fred Dixon sought to achieve seem so unremarkable today that the opposition he encountered strikes us as ludicrously obstructive. To be fair the funds available were never sufficient, but he regarded his struggles as a campaign against the attitudes of entrenched authority.

Send and Ripley History Society believes the memoirs to be a valuable contribution to social and local history. The views expressed by the author, however, are not necessarily those of the Society.

These memoirs provide an absorbing insight into village life and a glimpse within its hierarchy. They also reveal a purposeful and determined man who cared deeply about his work, the children he taught and the community he served. This is especially evident in his evocative account of the war years which will stir the memories of those who lived in Ripley through the period.

Send & Ripley History Society.

Preface

Most of us I suppose can turn back the pages of our lives and point to some critical moment when, as a result, our lives were altered in some way or other, but how many can turn to an apparently trivial occurrence and say "That was responsible for a decision of vital importance made in later life". I will relate such an incident and the effect it had on a choice I once made.

In August 1901 as a small boy aged five years, I distinctly remember my mother taking me one Sunday afternoon to see the Surrey Yeomanry in camp in the field near the sewage beds below Ranmore Common. The previous night there had been a severe thunderstorm and the horses picketed on lines in the open field had stampeded, but on that quiet Sunday afternoon everything was back to normal. The lines of tents, the horses with beautiful glossy coats and the Yeomen walking about with glistening spurs on their heels and the brilliant red fronts to their khaki tunics made a lasting impression on me. I wanted to be a Yeoman, but, alas, I was only five years old.

Each summer after that, troops of cavalry known as "Cubitt's Robins"[1] with red breasted tunics passed through the village on manoeuvres. I inspected all their shiny trappings, spurs, stirrups, bits and the white head-ropes, swords and rifles as they passed my point of vantage on the pavement. However unlikely it seemed then, I was, in fact, destined to ride that same road wearing similar uniform on one of those beautiful mounts.

I joined the Surrey Yeomanry in October 1914 just after the outbreak of the First World War. It was the beginning of a hazardous trek which lasted four and a half years, taking me to Egypt, Italy, France, Belgium and Germany.

Joining the Yeomanry turned out to be a crucial choice, for almost all my friends joined the (Woking) 7th Battalion, The Queens (Royal West Surrey Regt.), and were killed when the Battalion was decimated on 1st July 1916 at Carnoy during the first battle of the Somme. Later on in 1917 we also became infantry in the 10th Battalion, The Queens (Royal West Surrey Regt.), but the blood bath of the first Somme battle was then over. But for the effect of that Sunday afternoon walk I might have been on the Somme with my friends.

Instead I survived to enjoy 25 years as headmaster of Ripley School. That my recollections of those years are now recorded here is entirely due to the persuasion of my daughter Joan, and her husband, Brian Wilkins. Both being teachers themselves, they felt that the incidents I narrated to them were unique and could never recur; as the end of an era, they deserved to be placed on record. I have to thank my daughter for her constructive comments and I wish to express my gratitude to Mrs. Audrey Hunt (neé Bashall) who so ably typed my original manuscript.

Fred Dixon   March 1969

Now that publication of my story has become a reality I wish to express my thanks to the Send & Ripley History Society. I am deeply grateful to those individual members who have so painstakingly prepared my manuscript for the printer and I would not wish their labours to pass unnoticed.

Fred Dixon, August 1986

(1)   *Cubitt's Robins: The Surrey Yeomanry acquired the name from Col. The Hon. Guy Cubitt who commanded the regiment for a number of years before the First World War.*

Contents

Illustrations

Acknowledgements are due to the following for permission to reproduce certain of the illustrations:
Miss Winnie Blakeman
Mr. John Hutson
Miss Rose Onslow
Mr. Ken White.

Introduction

My first knowledge of Ripley was obtained through a board game which we enjoyed as a family. We had no radio or television or even electricity in our home but we had books and games. One game was known as "Wheeling". It was something like Snakes and Ladders. We played with cut out figures of cyclists which were moved on the throw of a dice. At one corner of the board was a picture of "The Angel" at Thames Ditton, and in the centre was "The Anchor" at Ripley. Between the two inns ran a highway, full of hazards for the unwary cyclist who had poor brakes and worn tyres. In real life the cyclists had regular weekend runs from "The Angel" to "The Anchor".

Towards the end of the last century "The Anchor" was kept by the Misses Dibble who were held in high esteem by the cyclists. I was told by a member of the Dibble family that when the cyclists were inside at the bar, one sister would bolt the doors while the other read the Bible to them. After the sisters died, the cyclists erected a memorial window to them in Ripley Church.

Ripley originally developed where an important east to west highway was crossed by a south to north track. Near the intersection in about the year 1160 a hospice or chapel was built for travellers. Around this building a community grew up which provided for the needs of the travellers as well as for the local people.

The condition of the main road must at times have been very bad and the advent of heavy wheeled traffic would have made it much worse. One has only to walk along an old drove road to imagine what it was like. Eventually, after the passing of a statute in 1749, turnpikes were established and the tolls paid for road maintenance. One such turnpike was constructed about a hundred yards from the "Jovial Sailor" on the Guildford side. I remember the turnpike house on the south side of the road at this point.

This road has been used by many famous people amongst whom were Charles I on his way to execution in London and the Duke of Monmouth for the same reason. Nelson and, one must suppose, Lady Hamilton also used the road. Dickens knew it well enough to deposit Nicholas Nickleby and Smike at a certain milestone on the top of Hindhead.

When I was a lad I lived in Send and I remember an occasional stage coach[1] passing through Ripley with the guard in the 'boot' blowing a

1

warning approach on his long horn. It must have been a regular service, even if it ran infrequently, because I walked from Send to Send Dip to see it pass. Many years later, Messrs. Watney, Combe and Reid, the brewers, from time to time ran a coach[2] drawn by four magnificent horses from London to Guildford. On one occasion on its return journey it stopped at the "Jovial Sailor" where the horses and passengers refreshed themselves – the horses with a nose bag of oats and chaff, and the passengers undoubtedly paid tribute to the brewery's products. When they were about to set out again for London, 'mine host' Mr. Waller 'phoned me and when this 19th century equipage passed the school it was given a rousing cheer from the children congregated in the playground for that purpose. Travelling at twelve miles per hour, the coachman waved his whip, the ladies in poke bonnets and 19th century dress all bowed, the gentlemen raised their grey toppers and the uniformed guard blew a fanfare on his trumpet.

Earlier travellers through the village were the gaggles of geese proceeding under their own power to market in London. Gertrude Jekyll described in her book "Old West Surrey", published in 1904, how yellow vans drawn by four horses, carrying fish from the coast to

2. *Reliving the coaching days by the Jovial Sailor.*

2

Billingsgate, often passed along the London road, but more uncommon fish carriers were the little carts drawn by dogs. "The dogs were big, strong Newfoundlands. Teams of two or four were harnessed together. The team of four would carry three to four hundredweight of fish, besides the driver. The man would 'cock his legs up along the sharves', as an old friend describes it, and away they would go at a great rate. They not only went as fast as the coaches, but they gained time when the coach stopped to change horses, and so got the pick of the market." Broom squires[3] from Hindhead were also seen with their carts loaded with besoms, peddling them as they travelled.

Lastly we come to the professional travellers, or 'tramps' as they were more often called. They were objects of suspicion all along their weary way between the workhouses in Kingston and Guildford, a distance of eighteen miles. They were unkempt, filthy in appearance, with clothing tied together with pieces of string and often with sacking wrapped over the remains of their boots. Their demeanour was usually morose and sullen. Today, very few of these social misfits pass through the village.

Although villages are surrounded by fields, how often does one come across a village possessing a playing field or open space for children? In rural areas children were often as badly catered for in this respect as children in some industrial areas. There would usually be a cricket pitch and a football ground for adult men – all the rest was arable land or down for grazing.

How fortunate then were the children of Ripley for they possessed one of the largest greens in the country; it constitutes that part of the common not enclosed as a result of the 1803 Act – in all about 65 acres. It used to contain a pond, had ample room for football and cricket pitches, and half the total area was rough common, where gorse and bracken flourished and provided a home for birds and rabbits and an occasional adder. "The old, gold common" – this is what the children imagined when reading A.A. Milne's 'Market Square'.

Some properties in Ripley had what were known as "Farren Rights"[4] entitling the occupiers to graze specific numbers of sheep etc. on the Green. The Green was controlled originally by the Lord of the Manor, Lord Onslow of Clandon Park, but in later years this duty was carried out by the Guildford Rural District Council. The farren holders had the right to veto propositions relating to the use of the Green, even if the R.D.C. offered no objections. During my time in

Ripley only one of the farren holders had cattle to graze but the right was never exercised by him.

One should never mention the Green without referring to its associations with cricket. As far as I know the first ever reference to cricket is found in the annals of the Guildford Royal Grammar School in 1598, and it could be that cricket has been played on Ripley Green since the 17th century. I have wondered if the fame of Ripley in the cricketing world of 1803 was responsible for such a large area being left for the use of the village when the commons were enclosed.

The Green was a nursery of Surrey cricket and has produced many good cricketers, the most famous of whom was Edward Stevens, commonly known as "Lumpy". Born in neighbouring Send, he played for the Ripley club, and in 1773 was playing cricket for Surrey and All-England.

In 1775 on the Portsmouth Artillery ground in a match between five of the Hambledon Cricket Club and five All-England players, the last Hambledon player was set to get fourteen runs with Lumpy bowling. He got them, but in the process Lumpy bowled three times through the wicket without dislodging the bail. This was considered unjust so the third stump was introduced. Further evidence of Lumpy's consistent bowling is to be found when his patron the Earl of Tankerville offered a wager of £100 that Lumpy would hit a feather on the pitch within four balls. He did it with his second! Lumpy died at the age of eighty-four and is buried in the churchyard at Walton-on-Thames.

The Green was also used for many other events. Shortly after the foundation of Newark Priory at the close of the 12th century, in return for a white palfrey (a pack horse), King Henry III granted a charter for a fair to be held at Ripley on the Eve of the Feast of St. Mary Magdalene which, in the modern calendar, falls on 22nd July. This fair, now about 750 years old, has continued to the present day, though probably not without some breaks. Certainly a few stalls kept it going during the Second World War. Fairs were usually held on the feast day of the saint to whom the local church was dedicated.

Guy Fawkes' Night is celebrated in Ripley by a fun fair and bonfire of such magnitude that it attracts visitors from miles around. After the Second World War it increased in popularity. Among the activities was the roasting of a pig over which Roger Brown officiated, and a display of fireworks enlivened the proceedings. Village merriment was not confined to fairs and bonfires. The populace was exceptionally responsive to days of national celebration when the Green became the

4

3. Maypole Dancing on Ripley Green
King George VI Coronation

4. Ripley C. of E. Primary School in its later days.

centre of most of the festivities, including children's and adults' races and country dancing by the school children around a Maypole.

The history of general education in Ripley really begins in 1847 with the opening of the National School, later the Church of England School. The two oldest classrooms, Rooms 2 and 3, were built in that year on what had been glebe land with materials similar to those used in reconstructing the nave of the church the year before. The last room to be added, Room 1, was built in 1897. It was known as the "Jubilee Room" to commemorate Queen Victoria's Diamond Jubilee.

Ripley Court School, a private institution, was established in the village in 1893 by Mr. R.M. Pearce, who transferred the school from Ealing. Ripley Court itself was probably built around 1700 by Nicholas Fenn whose tomb is to be found in the floor of the chancel in the church. He knew Samuel Pepys who may have visited him in the village on his way to Portsmouth. In the 1870's Ripley Court was owned by the wife of the Rev. Marshall who had a living in London but preferred to reside in Ripley. She was responsible for building a junior school in Rose Lane which is now the British Legion Club. The scholars there paid two pence a week to the governess. Seniors were sent to the school on the main road where they paid three pence weekly. Mr. Stephen

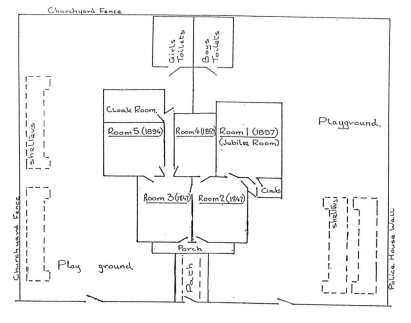

RIPLEY CofE ELEMENTARY SCHOOL
as in January 1936
(not to scale)

JS July 85

Bradley, who at one time was coachman to Dr. J.H. Sutcliffe, a local G.P., once told me that he remembered attending a Dame School when he was about five years old. This was in the house now called Turner's Cottage in Rose Lane and would have been around 20 years after the building of the National School.

There also used to be a private school for boys at Ryde House which backs on to the Green, founded in about 1880 by a Mr. T.M. Berridge. He was sartorially an outstanding figure in the village in his usual attire of black broad cloth trousers, frock coat, Gladstone collar, white bow-tie, top hat and elastic-sided boots. How could one hope to compete with that? He was later joined by Mr. Goodman, the father of Tom Goodman who became Clerk to the Parish Council. At a later date the school moved to new premises at the other end of the High Street, the site of which is now occupied by Gibbs, the agricultural engineers. Here it became known as Ryde House Commercial School and attracted the sons of prosperous farmers and trades-people in the area, as well as some overseas students. Before the First World War the school also started catering for girls who were accommodated in Newark Lane opposite the present entrance lodges to Dunsborough House. The school closed down about the year 1937. During the Second World War the Newark Lane building became a hostel for girls, and later for boys, who had been evacuated to the area and who proved difficult to handle. These children attended the Church of England school.

One other school was started in 1935, by a cafe proprietor. His business card showed his dual capacity as:–

Rio Cafe,	Rio School,
Proprietor,	Headmaster,
C. Allwork.	C. Allwork.

It did not last long! This reminds me of an advertisement I once saw in the columns of the 'Woking News and Mail'. It ran thus:– "Backward girl wanted to take a class of infants in exchange for tuition. Apply . . ."

(1)   This may have been the "Red Rover" coach which was driven in the 1890's by gentlemen whose hobby it was to drive four-in-hand. It had originally run from London to Southampton along this road until the service ceased in 1847. – Note by Matthew Alexander in Surrey Archaeological Society Bulletin No. 210 (April 1986).

(2) This was most likely the same "Red Rover", acquired in 1950 by Sanders Watney who ran it from London to Southampton at intervals between 1952 and 1963 – Ibid.

(3) Broom squires were basically squatters who lived by tying heaths into brooms (Shorter Oxford English Dictionary). There are references to them at Hindhead in Eric Parker's "Highways and Byways in Surrey" (1908). Sabine Baring-Gould published a novel entitled "The Broom Squire" in 1896. Charles Kingsley, who lived for 30 years until his death in 1875 in Eversley, Hampshire, another area renowned for broom squires, described the breed in "My Winter Garden".

(4) Farren rights were the ancient common rights of pasturage. The Send and Ripley Inclosure Act, 1803, provided that those possessing such rights should be allowed to pasture specific numbers of animals on the Green in respect of specific property. The Inclosure Award, completed in 1815 set out the persons, the numbers of which kind of animals and in some cases the properties concerned. It is believed that only the owners of Tudor House and Cedar House (together formerly comprising the George Inn), Dunsborough House and "Cobwebs" have successfully registered their rights under the Commons Registration Act, 1965.

Appointment and First Impressions

My involvement in Ripley started in 1935 when I, with half a dozen other hopeful candidates, assembled at Ripley C. of E. School in a squalid classroom. There were holes in the floorboards and very thin places which gave ominously where one walked.

After the interview we each had to re-enter the classroom next door where the Managers were assembled, call out our names, pause and return to the other classroom. This method of selection was apparently necessary so that personal images could be associated with the applications. I was most amused and this undoubtedly released the tension which we all felt, so I entered the room with a grin on my face. The vicar told me later that my grin had carried the day.

Mr. W. Blaxland, the retiring headmaster, had arranged to give me early notice of the result of the interview. School telephones were only to be found in Surrey Grammar Schools, so on Thursday of the following week at 10 a.m. I was to be in the public telephone kiosk at the end of Maybury Road, Woking, and he arranged to speak to me from the 'phone box in the centre of Ripley village. His call came through and he said "You can hang the flags out".

Two days later it was officially confirmed that I had been appointed headmaster of the school which then covered the full age range of pupils from 5 to 14. I was to commence on the 6th January 1936 at a salary of £437 per annum with a school house at 15 shillings (75p) per week.

My appointment was equally important to a colleague who was teaching in the same Woking Central school as myself. Before World War II women teachers in State schools were forced to resign on marriage but in C. of E. schools this rule could not be enforced. Mrs. Herrington, the colleague in question, wanted to marry but her future husband's financial position would not allow her to retire so she hoped to get a post in a Church school. Her opportunity came when I was appointed to Ripley and needed a Principal Woman Assistant. She had therefore been anxiously awaiting my return from the telephone kiosk.

Church schools at this time were usually found in villages and were generally old and ill-favoured buildings with no staff rooms or other facilities now considered essential. The buildings were the property of the Church and the external maintenance devolved upon the School

Managers. The teachers were appointed by the Managers but paid by the Local Education Authority. Text-books and equipment were also supplied by the Local Education Authority. At the time of my appointment the management consisted of four foundation members appointed by the Church, one representative from the County Council and one from the Parish Council. Of the six Ripley Managers only one was married and not one had attended a Church or State elementary school.

It will be seen as my story develops that my association with the Managers was mainly with Captain Christopher Pearce who at that time occupied the posts of Chairman, Treasurer and Correspondent, and the Vicar, The Reverend Morgan Evan Thomas. My predecessor warned me of the feud which existed between Captain Pearce and the Vicar.

My wife, Dorothy, immediately sensed difficulties. She said "You will have to be careful how you tread. If you side with one, the other will become a potential enemy". My reply was "I am going to plough a straight furrow and then if their furrows cut across mine it will be because theirs are not straight". She said "How will you know if yours is straight?". I reminded her that when a ploughman cuts a furrow he

6. *School group with Rev. Thomas and Wm. Blaxland*
(Fred Dixon's predecessor)

picks a point in the hedge at the other side of the field and goes straight for it. I finished by saying. "My target will be the welfare of the children". Most of my future difficulties arose from the fact that I did all in my power to put those words into deeds against great opposition.

Captain Pearce was one of two sons of Mr. & Mrs. R.M. Pearce who founded Ripley Court School. He also had a sister who married Mr. Guy Onslow, a relative of Lord Onslow and later headmaster at Ripley Court. Captain Pearce never married and was well known in the village. He would walk about in his deer-stalker's cloak, cap, plus fours and stout boots, and was never without his cromak[1]. He was a Justice of the Peace on the Woking Bench, Chairman of the Parish Council and a member of Guildford Rural District Council. He also had a considerable reputation as a local antiquarian and archaeologist, having published a distinguished report on his excavation of Newark Proiry[2].

The Captain's adversary, the Vicar, was also a bachelor. A fiery Welshman, he had had a distinguished army career during the First World War and had won the Military Cross. He held the living at Ripley from 1930 until 1953. Slightly built, he stood about 5 feet 7 inches tall and had sparse grey hair. His attitude towards people tended to be aggressive, which hardly helped him in his parochial duties. I have always felt that it showed he was ill at ease in ordinary society and he often told me that he was unfortunate in not having a wife to take his side in his many difficulties.

He had a foolish habit of trying to curry favour with small children when he met them in the street by tickling them until they collapsed on to the ground. In the end he had to come to me to stop the children calling after him in the street, "Silly old Vicar!"

The temperaments of the two protagonists, Captain Pearce and the Vicar, were as different as oil and water in that they would never mix. In addition they were virtual dictators in their own spheres. For example, the Vicar objected to the noise made by people's heels when they were walking to and from the altar rails at Holy Communion. To counter this he bought a large carpet which completely covered the pavement. The pavement, however, had been laid as a memorial to Mr. R.M. Pearce by his family! He had died tragically in a cycling accident.

The Captain was, as I have already said, acting as Chairman, Correspondent and Hon. Treasurer of the Ripley School Managers. He had taken over the chairmanship during the interregnum after the resignation of the previous Vicar, the Rev. Arnold Hope Wraith Headeach. Notwithstanding the fact that the incumbent was supposed to be the ex-officio Chairman, he refused to give up the chair to the Rev. Thomas.

The Managers were elected by the very few people who regularly subscribed to the school funds. There was no public invitation for people to subscribe except once a year when the Church collection amounting to only about two pounds ten shillings (£2.50) would be given.

The deadlock over the chairmanship was broken by the Vicar's indefatigable helper, Mrs. S. Methold. She had terrific strength of character and was profoundly religious. She became a subscriber and at once sat down and wrote to the National Society[3] asking pertinent questions relating to the trust deeds of the school. It was soon confirmed that the Vicar should be in the chair and as a result the Captain was forced to give it up.

I had seen the building and playground when I visited the school to be interviewed for the post of headmaster but I met the children for the first time on the day that school opened. Generally speaking, they were well dressed but I was not prepared to see the boys in the top class sitting at their desks collarless and with scarves round their necks and wearing muddy Wellington boots. This apparently was school uniform! I pointed out the desirability of wearing Wellingtons when walking to school along muddy paths and lanes, but as none of them appeared to wear them indoors at home, I said that they must change to indoor footwear when they reached school. This presented no difficulty. I made no rule about wearing collars, but every boy had to leave his scarf in the porch with his outdoor clothes. Evidently they felt rather naked round the neck for soon they all wore collars.

The basic work was good in spite of the many difficulties and my predecessor and his staff were to be congratulated on their efficiency. The senior girls went once a week to Cobham for cookery and the senior boys to Send for woodwork, travelling by public transport.

In addition to Mrs. Herrington, Principal Woman Assistant, who came with me from my Woking school, there was Mr. Hughes, a teacher from Wales, a natural musician and trainer of choirs. On November 20th 1936 a Senior Choir and a Junior Choir competed at the Woking Music Festival. The results were excellent, three certificates being obtained out of a possible four and the judge, Dr. Geoffrey

Shaw, remarked on the excellent quality of the singing. When Mr. Hughes returned to Wales, it was a great loss to the school.

Mrs. Doughty taught the Reception class and Miss Goldsmith, known affectionately as "Cottage Loaf", taught the Upper Infants. This appellation was given her because of her shape and proportions. She was about 5 feet 5 inches tall including her bun which was used for securing her hat to her head by two hat pins when she went out to "drill".

Mrs. Doughty left for family reasons and her place was taken by Miss Marsh, the daughter of a well known headmaster in Woking. In her case, too, the children employed their evident gift for finding suitable nicknames and she became "Marshmallow". She was adored by all the children.

7. School staff c. 1956.
Arnold Porter   Ruth Jones   Stan Pollard
June Westcott   Fred Dixon   Winifred Stoyle

(1)   A cromak is a walking-stick

(2)   Captain Pearce's report on his 1928 excavation of Newark Priory in Volume 40 of the Surrey Archaeological Collections is the *authoritative account of both the history and the buildings of the Priory. It was Captain Pearce who pointed out in the report the long-established error in the spelling of the surname of Ruald de Calna who, together with his wife, Beatrice de Sandes, jointly founded the Priory. (Earlier and some later books have the name incorrectly as de CALVA).*

(3)   The "National Society for the Education of the Poor according to the Principles of the Church of England" was founded by churchmen in 1811. The "National" or Church schools, of which Ripley was one, became the usual mode of popular education in the English village – C.M. Trevelyan "English Social History".

SIGHTING SHOTS

My first brush with Captain Pearce arose over involvement in voluntary activities. I knew that my predecessor had, like the Captain, been very active in this respect. I, however, wanted time to organise matters relating to the school and I was prepared with an answer when the Captain approached me. He wanted me to act as Hon. Secretary and Hon. Treasurer of Ripley Fire Brigade which was supported by voluntary contributions. I told him that I needed a year to settle down and suggested he ask me again after that if he thought I could still help.

The next I knew, twelve months later, was a request to attend the Fire Brigade Annual General Meeting at the Rio Cafe (now Ripley Transformers) on the very next evening. It could have been very inconvenient but I duly went and was formally introduced. Afterwards the Captain asked me to write up the minutes in rough for him to enter in the minute book. I thought this a strange request but, not wishing to cause friction, I complied.

Later on I discovered, on the counter in the Rio Cafe, copies of the Statement of Accounts for Ripley Fire Brigade with F. Dixon, Hon. Treasurer at the bottom. I had not handled any money nor had I seen any accounts. A year later the same thing happened again, after which I resigned!

When I arrived at the school, the only lighting was by means of antiquated gas burners and I had to provide the shillings (5p) for the slot meter. We were not allowed any petty cash in those days and I had to claim a refund periodically from the County Treasurer. The light the burners gave out was so bad that it was gloomier inside than out! In winter, towards the end of the afternoon session, needlework and other handicraft had to give way to oral lessons. Reading, except by the teacher, was quite out of the question. I must add that the buildings on either side of the school, the police station and the church, were both lit by electricity.

Because we had no display boards, whenever we wanted to display the children's work we had to stick it onto the distempered walls causing them to flake in many places. I wrote asking the Managers if they would consider fixing display boards. Some time later I received a reply saying they were not prepared to do this since it was considered to be the duty of the Education Committee. The Committee, however, considered that the Managers should be responsible. Result – stalemate. Strangely when I spoke to the Vicar he knew nothing about it. The matter had, apparently, not been brought before the Managers! Between us, we resolved things. The Vicar gave me some pieces of plywood that he happened to have stored in the roof of his garage and I spent a Saturday fixing them to the walls.

The school gardens were on a plot of land some distance from the school and on the far side of the police station. The plot stretched well back from the main road and when I took over I was told that the front half was to be used in the near future for police houses and the school gardens would be in the rear portion.

There were two snags to this arrangement which certainly increased my duties. One was that we had no access except through the garden of the police house. The other was that the land at the rear had never been cultivated and was overgrown with persistent weeds and brambles. It also contained the beehives of my predecessor who seemed to be in no hurry to move them. Every time we went to the gardens a boy by the name of Leonard Pullen came to me with the request that I extract a bee from his hair. He had red hair which he used to saturate in pungent Californian Poppy hair oil. Ultimately, I insisted that he wore a cap so that the bees would not again mistake him for a highly scented flower!

Commencing work on the rough but fallow land gave me plenty of scope for designing a school garden. I wanted a garden which could be used by all the children and not simply a number of rectangular plots for the senior boys to grow vegetables. I planned areas where the infants and juniors could plant flowers, herbaceous plots for the senior girls and plots of soft fruits. There were also three large experimental plots for the senior boys where they could grow vegetables and engage in a programme of rotation of crops. To complete the plan I prepared for a small lawn where lessons could be taken and notes made on the work which was being carried out.

In all this I had the "assistance" of eighty-years old Stephen Bradley who was employed as a gardener at Ripley Court. His presence was often inconvenient as I had to have him not to suit my timetable but when it was convenient for the Court to release him. I had arranged my timetable so that the gardening instruction came after the afternoon break. This reduced the caretaker's work because the soil from the boys' boots was no longer taken into the classroom.

I had roughly forty boys in the eleven to thirteen age group to work on the gardens which as already indicated were situated in a very inconvenient position. In the first place all the water had to be carried from the school. Secondly, I was often called away to interview somebody in school and my absence was occasionally unavoidably protracted. Sometimes when I returned to the scene of operations the air would be filled with missiles, such as would come easily to hand in a garden. I warned the combatants, indeed I erred in warning too often, for I did not wish to employ corporal punishment if it could be avoided. Once again it happened. I called the class together and told them that only a few days previously it had been reported in the Press that an irate father had taken a headmaster to Court because his son had had an eye knocked out under identical conditions. I told them that the parent lost the case and the boy lost his eye. It was my duty to see that none of them lost an eye and, in my own interests, to see that I was not brought before a Court because of their stupidity. I warned that it if happened again I intended to cane each boy who was taking part.

It did happen again. I collected the opposing forces, from which some had tried to slink away. I asked for any boy present who had not joined in the fracas to step to the front. There were some twelve or fifteen of them and they all remained where they were. I reminded them of my promise and marched them off to school. I lined them up and said "I am going to give each of you two across the seat. When you have had them you will stand up and say 'Thank you very much, sir'. That is because I have prevented you having you eyes knocked out". When the ordeal was over they were all grinning ruefully, and I was smiling when I said "Now let that be the end of it". It was. There was no more horse-play in my absence.

Shortly after I arrived in Ripley I received a curious communication. It was an anonymous letter threatening all sorts of things if I allowed "popish practices" to continue in school, and warning me against co-operating with the Vicar. I showed it to the Vicar and he said that he had had a similar letter. He seemed to have an idea it was from an old lady who did not live in the village, but was a relative of a well-known Ripley resident.

My relations with the Vicar and practices in school were not affected by the missive, but it does seem to have some bearing on what happened later. One day over a cup of tea in his study he said "Now that you have had time to settle down, I shall expect you to bring the whole school into church every Tuesday morning for Sung Eucharist". The regulations allowed me to take the children into church on seven occasions during the school year, and those occasions were to be shown on the school timetable. I explained this to him and said I was prepared to co-operate over and above that, provided that he had the written consent of the Surrey County Council.

The ball was back again in his court so he travelled to Kingston to see what concession he could extract from the Chief Education Officer. He was told that the Chief Education Officer would communicate with him in the near future and, quite naturally, the reply was sent to the school Correspondent, Captain Pearce.

Here was plenty of ammunition to shoot at the Vicar and in less than no time a meeting of the Managers was convened. "Who gave the Vicar the authority to interview the Chief Education Officer?". "By what authority did he demand the presence of the whole school in church every Tuesday for Sung Eucharist?". It was not shown on the school timetable as he the Captain knew, for he had countersigned it. What was worse in the Managers' eyes, it had been happening without their knowledge in my predecessor's time – or so it was said at the meeting. I cannot believe that two of the Managers who regularly attended Sung Eucharist did not know that the children were there.

The Vicar took his defeat like a sportsman and never held it against me. Thenceforth, by arrangement with the Vicar, the school attended Sung Eucharist on the seven permitted occasions – Ash Wednesday and the six Tuesdays following and this was shown on the school timetable. The Vicar was quick to notice the absence of my daughter, then about six years old, and he asked me why she did not attend. I told him that in my opinion Sung Eucharist was not a suitable service for children, but if he substituted a children's service he would see her there and possibly a few other children whose parents thought as I did. The following Lent a children's service was substituted.

Mrs. Methold's religious fervour was the driving force behind the annual Nativity plays for which she was famous. Her productions were excellent. The children taking part were well drilled and, with the exception of some of the costumes made by the parents, she had little assistance. The stage lighting effects were something that she could not cope with and these were attended to by Stuart Paice, the Scoutmaster.

Years went by and anno domini made things more difficult for her, so the Vicar decided to ask for voluntary help from the audience. Two women volunteered to assist in the production of future plays. They were an aged mother and her daughter and both had been associated with the stage. They were well qualified to do the job but as time went on it became clear that the co-producers were incompatible. The daughter started a group for the village girls to learn ballet dancing. They were known as the "Ripley Belles". When they were comparatively proficient a show was staged in the Church Hall. I did not attend, but from all accounts the producer of ballet had done a remarkable job in a short time and everybody praised the venture. Miss Marsh who had charge of the Reception Class in school also produced Nativity plays. They were not polished, the costumes were make-shift and the performers worked to no script - they 'ad libbed' for all they were worth but they lost nothing in sincerity. On one occasion, Mary was sitting nursing baby Jesus when the door opened and in staggered Joseph with a bag of tools over his shoulder. "Oh Joseph" said Mary, "I'm so glad you've come. Jesus has been a perfect little devil today!".

8. *The School Play: A Midsummer Night's Dream*

THE VILLAGE SCENE

"The rich man in his castle,
The poor man at his gate,
God made them high or lowly
And ordered their estate".

Hymns A. & M.

Until recent years the people in rural areas, in southern England at least, were conditioned to the sentiments expressed in the above verse. Those were the ideas with which I grew up and, in the same way, the more privileged members of society accepted their status as God given.

When I was a boy the pattern of seating in a village church was as follows:- The members of the patron's family frequently sat in the chancel behind the choir stalls; the gentry occupied the centre block of pews in the nave; the tradesmen and their wives and families on the north side of the church, and the domestic staff at the back. If there happened to be a Children's Home or Boarding School in the village, they sat on the south side. This pattern of seating may still be found in some rural churches.

When I reached Ripley I found much that was feudal, but the people were stirring from their long sleep. I think that the education of the masses, inadequate though it was, was the cause of this awakening. Other people were uneasy for a different reason. Education was responsible for people having ideas which were inconsistent with their way of life.

Before applying for the post at Ripley, I had applied for the post of headmaster of Albury C. of E. School. Albury was the home of the Duke of Northumberland and the living was in his hands. The Vicar of Albury and the Managers, which included the Duke's agent, were seated round a table in the village hall. I was led into the room and asked to be seated. The first question put to me by the Vicar was more in the nature of a statement. "Of course, you are a Conservative, Mr. Dixon?" I replied that politics were not taught in the elementary school. He responded, "No, I know, but we want to be sure that we don't appoint somebody who will teach Communism to the children". I replied that my views were quite moderate and that I was not an extremist to the right or to the left. There was an amusing irony to the conclusion of this story since the man appointed was far left. I wonder what he told them? I reported the matter to the National Union of Teachers who took the matter up, and the Managers' knuckles were rapped for bringing politics into the appointment.

Soon after my arrival in Ripley, a meet of the local harriers was held there. On the Saturday in question, my wife and daughter took our dog Shep into the village on a shopping expedition. I was working in the garden when I heard a clamour of barking close at hand, and I imagined that our peace-loving Shep had fallen foul of half a dozen other dogs. I ran to the garage, picked up a six foot length of two by two and sallied forth. To my amazement, and indignation, I saw a man in a green coat and white cord breeches bursting through the privet hedge which surrounded my garden, and he was followed by a pair of beagles. I intercepted him and demanded to know by what right he had broken through my hedge and walked across my garden. "We are after a hare" he replied. I told him that if people wished to enter my property I expected them to come in by the proper gate and then only with my permission. He said "I'm afraid that's not possible where the hare is concerned". "Never mind about the hare," I replied. "Get out!" and he went.

The hare was subsequently torn apart in the field opposite as my wife and daughter returned from the village, and they saw what took place. I was bursting with indignation and declaimed upon the beastliness of it all. However, although the law of trespass may have been on my side, I was in a tied school house and paid my rent to the Managers. Under similar circumstances, other villagers would not care to risk their livelihood. At Assembly I told the children what had happened and said I hoped they would not copy the bad example of people who should have known better.

Another incident reflects the same idea. Each Ascension Day the school was closed and the children assembled in the playground. At 8.50 a.m. they were crocodiled into church next door. On the first occasion I discovered that Ripley Court School was there in force and that they occupied all the seats in the body of the nave, leaving empty pews only under the organ loft at the back of the church and in the south aisle for my children. This would never do, so, at the close of the service I went to see the Vicar in the vestry. I told him that unless he made some other arrangements, I did not intend bringing the children another year. I finished by reminding him that Ripley children would not take second place to any school in their own church. The following year the schools sat side by side. I am quite sure that nothing high-handed had been intended. It was just something that some people took for granted without thinking, assuming that the hewers of wood and drawers of water should be in their proper place. This was also the line of thinking of some of the older villagers. Once during the course of a gardening lesson, I overheard the husky voice of my aged gardening assistant saying. "Which one of you *boys* was talking to them young *gen'l'men* over the wall last night?" (referring to the boys of Ripley Court School). "I was, Mr. Bradley" said Cyril Freeman, a very bright village boy. "Well, you look out or you'll be getting yourself into trouble". I joined in the conversation by enquiring if there was some infection at the Court. Boys and young gen'l'men indeed!!!

During World War II, there were troops stationed on local anti-aircraft sites, and their officers canvassed those people in the village who possessed baths to ascertain if their men could come for a bath on a fixed evening of the week – air raids permitting. In concert with other fortunate people, my wife and I offered the use of our bath. When a very well-off parishioner heard of the arrangement, she expressed horror at the thought of the rank and file using her bath. She was prepared to offer the use of her bath to commissioned ranks but not to privates.

During the 1939-45 war, the Bishop of Guildford started a Challenge Fund for a multiplicity of purposes. One was to complete the cathedral as soon as building could re-commence, another was to build Church schools, and yet another was to enable the stipends of the clergy to be increased. I wholeheartedly supported all of these, not necessarily in that order of priority. Two representatives came from the Diocesan Board of Finance to explain the scheme. The audience consisted mainly of lower middle class and poor people. The speakers were Mr. Fairbank Smith and a cleric whose name I have forgotten. They stressed the importance of the various items to be supported. The reference to the stipends of the clergy had my warmest support and then one of the speakers dropped a brick. He said it was essential for the stipends to be increased, especially as the clergy were unable to educate their children. Here was the serpent of privilege rearing its head again. At question time I agreed that the stipends should be raised considerably, but I said that I considered it an un-Christian act to come to a poor village where practically everybody had been to a Church or State school and ask for money to educate the clergy's children privately. Give them larger stipends, but do not use the educating of the clergy's children as a reason for doing so. There was no reason at all why they should not send their children to the church schools which they advocated for other people's children. I added that if that had been the case in the past, the church schools would be in a far better state of repair than they were at that time.

I was thanked for my suggestion.

HEAT AND LIGHT (Let there be....)

During my time at Ripley two part-time caretakers served the school before 9 a.m. and after 4 p.m. but anything requiring attention during school hours had to be carried out by the teaching staff. In the winter months this included seeing to the heating in the five classrooms, three of which had open fireplaces.

From 1st November to 31st March of every year recordings of the outside temperature and of each classroom were made at 9 a.m. and 2 p.m. These were entered on special forms and sent on the last school day of each month to County Hall. I cannot say what happened to them on arrival, but I suspect that a junior clerk filed them immediately.

All the classrooms were built like barns, no ceilings and with louvres in the roof. These louvres had to be closed in winter to prevent the loss of heat and, when the air cooled, it caused a down-draught in the areas of the room where there were no radiators. The coldest rooms were the oldest – Rooms 2 and 3; and Room 5, which was used by the infants, came a close second. The only way for the infants to keep warm was to group themselves round the open fireplace with its tall, iron guard. In that classroom I put two thermometers so that the different temperatures could be noted, one where the children sat and one away from the fire.

In very cold weather the thermometers in Rooms 2 and 3 frequently hovered round the 40°F (4.5°C) mark. When that was the case the children had to sit in their overcoats and gloves. The Surveyor's Department always received particulars relating to these temperatures, but nothing had ever been done about it. The Managers must have been aware of the situation as I came across an entry in an old Log Book in my predecessor's handwriting : "This day, the two classrooms nearer the main road are exceptionally cold. It is impossible to maintain an essential degree of heat and the children are sitting in their overcoats". It is doubtful whether the fathers of the children would have tolerated these conditions for themselves at their places of employment. The first thing I did was to bring in my own Valor Perfection oil stove and use it, surrounded by a fireguard, in Rooms 2 and 3 alternately.

At this time there was talk of building a new C. of E. Secondary School for the scholars of Send, Ripley, Ockham and East and West Clandon. The then Bishop of Guildford visited Ripley to address a meeting urging people to give financial aid. The sponsors of the plan, of whom my predecessor was one, were present, as well as the Managers of the contributing schools. It seemed to me an excellent opportunity to bring to the notice of the ecclesiastical authorities that things were far from being up to standard in the existing church schools. I protested against the church embarking on a building programme when the existing primary schools were in such a parlous condition.

The Church support for the School Fund then amounted to about £2.10s.0d. (£2.50p) annually as the result of one collection in church. The new school would want at least £20 annually from the Parish then and more than double that in later years. Knowing this, there were people in the village prepared to go forward with plans for a new C. of E. Secondary school. The sum of my resentment will not be fully understood until the reader has finished reading the whole record.

Seated in the audience at the meeting was a friend of the Vicar, Mrs. Hollingsworth from Hook Heath in Woking. She was connected with the well-known Oxford Street firm of Bourne and Hollingsworth and as a result of my protest offered to install a modern and more efficient boiler. This kind offer was accepted by the Managers and, as a result, the temperatures in Rooms 2,3 and 4 improved slightly, but they were not yet adequate.

I was tremendously encouraged by Mrs. Hollingsworth's generosity, but the gift which I valued most of all from her was her offer to pay for the wiring of the school for electricity. Every afternoon I had closed school with "Lighten our darkness we beseech thee O Lord", and here, in one respect at least, was the answer to my prayer.

The Vicar gave the order to the Woking Electricity Supply Company to wire the school for light and power. However, when the work was completed the Captain refused to sign the essential agreement necessary for connection to the mains. So here was a school building with obsolete gas supplies and fittings wired for electricity but with no power. Was there ever a more ridiculous state of affairs? The ball was now in the Vicar's court, but it was Mrs. Hollingsworth who retrieved it.

24

Some fifteen months later my prayers were really answered. Electricians from Woking came, joined the school to the mains, tested and left. In accordance with custom and in all sincerity, I reported to the Captain that every lighting point was working satisfactorily. To my surprise he wrote asking me who had given the order for the link up. I knew nothing about it and I told him that I thought he had. The Captain called an immediate meeting of the Managers. The Vicar was carpeted, but he said that the only order he had given was for the wiring of the building.

I can now relate what actually happened. Mrs. Hollingsworth was a very determined person. She stood no nonsense from anyone. When she saw how her generosity was being treated she decided to act on her own and went direct to the Chief Education Officer in Kingston. Thus the school had light and power and in more ways than one our gloom was dispelled. With electricity in the school we could now use the 'Radio Broadcasts for Schools' – if only we had a radio set ! That was my next target and again we found some friends.

To while away the tedious hours whilst waiting for air-raid warnings, the wardens in the A.R.P. (Air-Raid Precautions) post on the Green built up a 'kitty' and while entertaining themselves they also provided creature comforts. When they knew that I needed a radio set but had not the wherewithal to buy one, they kindly donated £10 for that purpose. I selected a second-hand one in Kingston, but could not buy it as regulations required the approval of the Surrey Education Committee which was not forthcoming. Instead I bought a film strip projector and an epidiascope with money raised by concerts plus the £10 from the A.R.P. wardens. The local Ann Haynes' Charity [1] also made a grant which enabled me to purchase a 6ft x 6ft portable screen for use with the projector.

But still I had no radio for the school ! For two or three years the Ripley Fire Service under Harry Hacker had raised funds to provide the Ripley children with Christmas parties. After a time they decided to dispose of the surplus funds and came to me for suggestions. My wife suggested that the monies could be used in the interests of the children if they bought a radio set for the school. The Fire Service thoroughly approved of this idea and shortly afterwards an up-to-date radio-gramophone set was purchased costing £60 and I was given £10 for maintenance.

A few weeks later the County Inspector arrived. I whipped off the covering to the set and asked him if he would like to listen to the tone.

25

He said "I thought I said you were not to buy one". I replied, "I haven't; I have had it given to me". I demonstrated its tone and he said, "I've never heard a better".

(1) By her Will dated 16th January, 1702, Ann Haynes gave to the Minister and Churchwardens of the Parish of Send (which then included Ripley) £300 to buy land so that the income from it could be used to put poor men's children to apprentice. The land was finally sold in 1947 for £3,000 and the money invested in Government Stock. The income is still distributed.

SANITATION AND ACCOMMODATION
(Room for improvement....)

When I commenced my new duties in 1936 my two part-time caretakers, Mr. and Mrs. Gunner, were together paid twenty shillings weekly and they had to provide their own soap and cleaning materials. An iron saucepan which held a quart substituted for a boiler to heat all the water required for scrubbing throughout. The saucepan was heated on one of the open grates or on a gas ring. Mrs. Gunner also washed all roller towels and blackboard dusters for no extra remuneration. Is it any wonder that the place was grimy and is it any wonder that morale suffered? I requisitioned a portable iron boiler on wheels with a built-in furnace and detachable flue.

My next target was the toilets, but when I suggested to the Vicar that he should bring the matter up before the Managers, he writhed like a soul in torment and said that he couldn't discuss the matter in mixed company!

It is necessary to turn to the plan of the school to understand my requirements. It will be seen that the playgrounds completely surrounded the main building with two dividing fences down the front and a dividing wall 6ft.6ins. high at the rear to separate the boys' playground and toilets from those of the girls! This meant that the senior and junior girls, in order to reach their toilet from Rooms 1 and 2, had to cross the boys' playground to the public footpath on the main road and enter the

26

9. William Gunner, school caretaker, with his grandaughter, Florrie

gate to the girls' playground and so to the toilets at the rear of the school. Similarly, the lower junior boys in Room 3 had to follow the same route in reverse. In bad weather this was not practicable and Rooms 2 and 3, or Rooms 2 and 4, functioned as corridors. Imagine the effect on the children and staff with these constant interruptions.

At this time the fund for the C. of E. Secondary school had been launched and it was also a time of particular managerial inactivity, so I called at the Vicarage and again asked the Vicar to do something about the toilets. I had already been to County Hall and spoken to Mr. R. Beloe, the Deputy Education Officer. I said that I did not intend to send my daughter to Ripley school unless the lavatories received a good deal of attention. I also told him that I had known children go home in pain rather than use them. He replied "What isn't good enough for your daughter is not good enough for other people's children". I concurred. Nothing was done, and no medical officer visited to corroborate my statements. I am positive that the Surrey Education Committee did not wish to tangle with the Church over the matter.

I told the Vicar what I had told Mr. Beloe, and I pointed out what a bad effect it would have on the Secondary School Building Fund if I refused to send my daughter to the village school because of the condition of the toilets. He said "What do you want?". My first requirement was that a gap should be knocked in the dividing wall at the rear of the school which would save the children having to use the public pathway on their way to the toilets. It would also ease the pedestrian traffic through the classrooms during inclement weather and enable the caretaker to move directly from one lavatory to the other without having to walk through the school.

To understand my other requests it is essential to know more about the lavatories. The girls' lavatories consisted of two rows of cubicles with four on one side of a passage and three on the other side, with a twenty-five gallon automatic flushing tank over each side. They worked on the principle of a syphon and were filled from a running tap over each tank. The faster the inflow, the more frequent the flushing. The minimum number of infants and junior and senior girls using six toilets was one hundred; the seventh toilet was reserved for women staff.

The boys' toilets consisted of a urinal on one side of the passage, flushed by a small syphon container – when it worked. On the other side of the passageway were three cubicles, of which one was reserved for male staff. The minimum number of junior and senior boys using these toilets was seventy. In order to increase the toilets available for boys Miss Farr, one of the Managers, suggested that the one used by the male staff should be used by the boys. "In that case", I said, "I shall use the toilet at home".

The boys' toilets were flushed by one automatic twenty-five gallon tank. All cubicles had box seats which extended the full width of the cubicles from the front of the pan to the wall at the back. The seats were worm-eaten and continually saturated. I said that I wanted all the seats ripped out and replaced with individual tip-up seats, with a small one for the infants.

The Vicar personally undertook to have the work done, and in the Parish Magazine of September 1938 was this report by the Vicar: "Owing to the fact that there had been no Managers' meeting held for the last eight months, the Chairman of the Managers and the Headmaster took upon themselves certain improvements which seemed to be very necessary. One of the classrooms was very dingy and dull. This has now been given a coat of sunlight colour and it has now become the brightest room in the school. (Author's Note:- The school

28

staff paid for this to be done instead of subscribing to the building of St. Bede's school). For many years past, the Headmaster has agitated for a door to be placed between the playgrounds for the benefit of the children. This has been erected and does away with the necessity of the children running round on to the road. The work has entailed the expenditure of nearly £8. The money was collected by Mr. Dixon, and we are most grateful to those who gave subscriptions to defray the expense. Those who are interested would be very welcome to come and inspect the work that has been done". Nobody came.

The gap in the wall was made and a door fitted. The lavatory seats were pulled out and the effect was shocking. Stretching from back to front and from side to side, to the depth of six or seven inches was a mass of stinking, wet soil. The contractor was asked to burn the wooden seats and cart away the soil. To complete the operation I requisitioned some hose and fittings so that the caretaker could daily swill the floors round the pedestals.

Things worked well until the children stayed to school meals. At midday there was nobody on the premises to increase the flow of water into the flushing tanks for peak hour use, so the inflow had to be adjusted as if the peak period lasted all day. From 9.0 a.m. to 4.0 p.m. 225 galls an hour was flushed, i.e. 1575 gallons went down the drain. No wonder I received a letter from the Chief Financial Officer asking me to reduce the amount of water used.

Nothing could be done about it until we had either a full time caretaker or individual flushing had been fitted. The latter was effected when the school became "controlled" after the 1944 Education Act. Lighting was also added, but not until after my retirement were the toilets heated. This was brought about throughout the County by a prolonged spell of exceptionally cold weather.

Before the advent of heating, such long spells of very cold weather brought difficulties in that the toilets froze and remained thus. The water in the pipes and in the pans was frozen solid. Salt had no effect. They could only be kept going by the caretakers burning braziers of coke all night. They went out before morning, but they usually did the trick. The braziers were made from old oil drums with holes knocked in the sides with a pickaxe. If the weather became very severe the braziers were in use during the day and were then protected by fireguards.

For one period during the war I had to rely on the services of two women part-time caretakers and, unfortunately, it coincided with an extremely prolonged cold spell. They could not cope with the braziers and my Valor Perfection oil stove made little difference. I was on the point of asking for the school to be closed when help came from an unexpected source. Mr. Les Morris had heard through his daughter of our difficulties and he offered to free the toilets of ice and get them flushing again. I gratefully accepted his kind offer and he spent a day at this distasteful and self-imposed task. I reported to the Managers upon the work he had done but the only thanks came from me. My sincerity, I hoped, would make up for the omission by the Managers.

What a time that was. Owing to the war, we were unable to obtain toilet rolls, and paper squares from newspapers had to be cut and strung up in the toilets. I wrote a letter to the National Union of Teachers. Questions were asked in Parliament and arrangements were made for supplies of paper-making material to be available for the manufacture of toilet rolls for schools.

The question of additional school accommodation also became an urgent issue when the Georgelands Estate was being built after the war. The Managers did not concern themselves with this matter so I went to the Clerk of the Works on the estate to find out how many houses were to be erected. Then I wrote to the Divisional Education Officer in Woking and told him that I would need extra space. His deputy, who replied, did not agree with my figures and said that the existing accommodation would be adequate. At this time I only had four classrooms at my disposal as Room 4 had been converted into a kitchen for school meals. He probably based his figures on my wartime numbers when I had two hundred and twenty in the school and thirty in the Church Hall.

However, I was sure of my facts and as it turned out extra accommodation was needed even though two classes were 50 plus and the other two 40 plus. The deputy Divisional Education Officer asked me to look round the village for a suitable hall. I found one, of sorts, at the rear of the Methodist Church. It was small, dark and cluttered with furniture. Electric light was needed all day, even in summer. There was a toilet and a stone sink. All furniture which was not needed was stacked against the rear wall, and the usable furniture consisted of trestles and table tops. At most it would accommodate twenty-eight.

When we brought the children over to the hall, we found that the forms on which they had to sit were too low and the tables too high so that the children wrote with their shoulders up near their ears. There were no pegs for the children's clothes and they had to be stacked on the furniture at the back. Imagine what it was like when the clothes were wet. When the teacher wrote on the blackboard, the lights in the front of the class had to switched off because the board reflected them so that the writing could not be seen.

The one toilet was useful for emergencies, but at play-time both girls and boys trooped 150 yards across the Green to the public conveniences. Here again there was a snag as on two occasions I had to write to the Guildford R.D.C. to have the walls whitewashed to cover up the graffiti. To reach the main school building, the class had to use a "Zebra" pedestrian crossing. On one occasion Mr. Porter, one of our masters, was standing on the crossing, holding his cycle with one hand and using the other to control the class. The children were half way when a car which passed over the crossing made them halt. Mr. Porter told me and I informed the police who took the case to court but to no avail.

Present day teachers looking at the plan of the school will immediately ask, "Where is the stock room?" and "Where is the staff room?". We had neither. Staff rooms were never considered essential when the early Church schools were built. Teachers who lived at a distance brought sandwiches and at lunch time met with other members of the staff in one classroom and ate their meal there.

SAFETY MATTERS

In law a teacher is considered to be in loco parentis and his, or her, actions are compared with those of a prudent parent. To be on the safe side of the law, therefore, a teacher has to be as imaginative and efficient as a super-parent. Mr. Justice Geoffrey Lane has laid down that in the modern conditions of large State schools the standard must be high. The teacher has "To take all reasonable and proper steps to prevent any of the pupils from suffering injury from inanimate objects, from the action of their fellow pupils, or from a combination of the two".

It is reasonable to assume that the above also applies to small Church schools. The headmaster or headmistress is in a particularly vulnerable position, inasmuch as the safety of all pupils on the register has to be considered. I imagine that if danger was foreseen from a source over which the Head had no control, some, if not all, of the responsibility could be passed on to the management or the Local Education Authority, as the case may be. Accidents will always happen, but once inside the school gate the onus is on the head teacher to see that accidents are minimised. What about the playground? The manhole covers? Are there any dangerous gratings to drains ?

I conducted a quick survey and found much that would have to be reported to the Managers. I shall never be able to understand why the headmaster was placed in the position of having to cause trouble between himself and his Managers. Surely the matter should have been dealt with at a higher level?

The playground which the girls and infants used was a hotch-potch of earth and broken tarmac. Many years before, it had had a tarmacadam surface all over to a depth of about two inches. It was now largely broken up leaving the soil exposed. Lumps of tarmac with sharp jagged edges projected and dotted the playground throughout. In wet weather the rain collected on the surface of the soil making the playground unusable. As the rain drained away it turned to mud and when frost was thawing out it was worse than ever. Children were continually tripping over the broken tarmac and teachers were kept busy binding wounds. I wondered why the Chief Financial Officer did not send me a chit querying the amount of first aid materials used!

The climax came when Connie Wanbon, the daughter of a policeman, fell and badly cut her chin. Dr. Creet said that the wound should be stitched, but as the child objected I left the matter in the hands of her parents. This incident gave me a reason for reporting to the Managers on the dangerous state of the playground. I pointed out that in the interests of the children and themselves I had put the playground out of bounds. All children, boys, girls and infants, had to use one playground and this necessitated re-drafting the timetable for the school so that each group occupied the playground at different times,

A year passed and nothing was done by the Managers. Under these crowded conditions it was inevitable that balls would go over the 6ft. high wall and prove to be a nuisance to the police family next door. On one occasion a ball landed in the baby's pram and on another descended amongst some crockery on the draining board. I reported this to the Managers and asked if they would have a wire netting guard fixed to the top of the wall separating the properties. Miss Farr said, "Need they play with balls in the playground?".

Again nothing resulted, so I requested permission to get a working party of old boys and fathers together to break up the remaining tarmac in the other playground and clear it and level the surface. To this idea the Managers were responsive, because it would not cost them anything.

I had a splendid response from the parents and working on two Saturdays we cleared and levelled the site. Jugs of beer from "The Anchor" helped to oil the wheels and I felt that it was a good investment. Once again the thanks of the management were absent. Instead, thanks were supplied by the children who enjoyed having their playground returned to them.

Inside the school was a passage which was floored with red and black tiles. Over the years, the red tiles had worn into holes while the black ones remained almost intact. I once twisted my ankle extremely badly and decided to draw the attention of the Managers to the condition of the passage. I asked to have it floated with cement. The Managers said that I must walk more carefully! When the school became "Controlled" the work was carried out by the Local Education Authority.

Vibration from traffic on the main road was responsible for the gable end of Room 2 leaning outwards at the top. Ridging and roofing tiles had pulled apart and on the inside the keystone over one window had dropped about 1¼ inches. Children were seated immediately beneath this window. My predecessor had considered the roof dangerous and he had given orders to the children in that room to get beneath their desks if they heard a noise coming from the ceiling. This advice had not been entered in the Log Book so I could not quote an entry when writing to the Managers.

I also considered the situation dangerous and reported to the Captain. I then drew the desks away from the area, roped it off and put a blackboard on an easel within the confines. On the board I printed in large letters DANGER-KEEP OUT! I was outside the school the next day seeing the children across the road when a car passed. I recognised the driver as Mr. Rutherford, the school inspector. I managed to attract his attention and he drew up. I asked him if he would spare me a few minutes. After showing him the keystone he said "That's dangerous. Don't let anybody sit within 6 feet of it. I am reporting this to the Chief".

The following day the Chief Inspector, Mr. Heath, came. He took a quick look and said, "This must be seen to at once". The Vicar, who at that time was not Chairman, was taking a lesson in the next room, so I suggested that Mr. Heath could speak to him. The Vicar said he could not help and advised Mr. Heath to see Captain Pearce. This he was unable to do and he had to be content instead with leaving a message for the Captain to the effect that the roof must receive immediate attention and stated his intention of returning in two weeks.

Exactly two weeks later Mr. Heath returned and once again the poor Vicar had to bear the brunt of Mr. Heath's anger when he discovered that his directions had been ignored. He finished by saying that if nothing was done within three weeks, the grant would be withdrawn and he was likewise informing Captain Pearce. The window soon received attention and the gable was braced.

Each year the School Medical Officer sent me a notice of an inspection of school buildings. Each year the same doctor came, and each year she reported upon matters of sanitation and hygiene, which could only be remedied by the Managers. Each year at the conclusion of her visit she said to me, "I am sending in a stinking report", to which my reply was, "Quite fitting". Nothing ever happened about these reports and they probably suffered the same fate as my temperature records.

The windows of the two oldest rooms, 2 and 3 which faced the road, and of Room 4 were different from those in the rest of the school. They had long frames about 3ft. 6ins. high and 1ft. 6ins. wide and swung on a pivot halfway along the long side. A rope fastened to a ring top and bottom enabled the window to be opened by pulling the top inwards and fixing it in position by means of a few turns around a cleat at the bottom of the window frame. These windows stuck in wet weather when the wood swelled. Dual desks were placed right against the wall which meant that the window could only be opened by the teacher climbing on an occupied desk, or by a child sitting next to the window.

One day the atmosphere of the room holding forty-five children became oppressive and the teacher told the nearest boy to open the window. He tugged on the rope but the window refused to yield. He got on to the seat of his desk and pulled again and still the window would not budge. "Give it a good tug!" said the teacher. The obedient child did. There was a pause followed by a shattering of glass, and there was the boy with his head through the window and the window frame draped round his shoulders. To say that the boy, the teacher and the class were surprised is far short of the truth. They were dumbstruck and when they all realised that no blood had been shed the tension gave way to laughter after the boy's head had been released from its restricting confines.

34

During the school term prior to the commencement of my duties in Ripley, Daniel Baker, a little boy aged nine, had been knocked down and seriously injured by a car as he was crossing the main road to get to school. When I saw the account of the accident in the "Woking News and Mail", I said to my wife, "I intend to do everything that is possible to see that no harm comes to any child while I am at Ripley". This was no easy task as at that time the school fronted the main London to Portsmouth road which had been referred to as the busiest road in the country by the county police authorities.

I first made an order that no child leaving school was to cross the road unaccompanied by an adult. They were told that if I was not there, they were to fetch me or wait until I came. At this stage I did not invite the staff to assist me because it was not incumbent on them (or me) to see the children across. In fact there was no need to say anything to the staff, as they followed my lead and co-operated wholeheartedly.

There was also no difficulty in getting the co-operation of the senior children. I pointed out that although they themselves were capable of crossing the road without any harm coming to them, their younger brothers and sisters were not. If the youngsters saw their senior brothers and sisters disobeying the order they might follow suit and a resultant accident would be their responsibility.

As a precautionary measure, I ordained that children should not congregate outside the entrance to the playground. One day, a car coming from London struck a lorry travelling in the opposite direction a glancing blow. The car turned over three times and finished upside down on the pavement at the school gate. The inside of the car was covered in blood and the driver was lying there unconscious. The children had just finished their meal and were running about the playground. I sent them all back into school with orders to the staff to keep them from the windows. We turned the car back over, got the man out and he was taken by ambulance to Guildford hospital.

The next job was to look about for some official assistance in the matter. I was prepared to do it myself, but there were two objections to that. The traffic was so dense that one could rarely find a gap through which the children could pass. This meant that the traffic had to be held up for that purpose and it was not lawful for me to do that. Secondly, it was beyond the terms of my engagement to see the children across. In other words, it was not part of my duty to see that they arrived home safely, and if an accident happened while I was holding up the traffic I could not look to the Surrey County Council for legal aid – I should be on my own.

In the first place I wrote to Captain Pearce but I also visited the police sergeant to see if I could get some official help unofficially. The sergeant, who had a daughter at the school, was sympathetic and to some extent helpful. He explained that his allotment of constables would not allow him to make a "point" outside the school at the time required, but he would give instructions that if any of the men were in the vicinity of the school when I was seeing the children across they were to take over. It was as much as I could expect under the circumstances and I gratefully accepted the offer, but it did not completely meet my requirements. Next I wrote to the Chief Education Officer, to Sir John Jarvis the then local Member of Parliament, and to the Royal Society for the Prevention of Accidents. I drew a blank each time. I then wrote to Mr. James Chuter Ede, M.P., who was also the Secretary for the Federation of Surrey Teachers in the National Union of Teachers. He held a unique position being both master and servant of teachers. I reported what I was doing and that I needed official assistance. He replied telling me to discontinue what I was doing as it was in excess of my duties and I would have to accept complete responsibility for any accident which might occur. In my reply I told him that I was in the position of a man walking along a river bank and seeing a child drowning. There was no legal liability for me to effect a rescue, but there was a moral responsibility which one had to accept. He then suggested that I should communicate with the parents, explaining the position, saying that I was prepared to see to the safety of the children without accepting responsibility for anything that might happen. This I did.

It is possible that my requests in high places may have started the ball rolling because about this time a suggestion was made at County Hall that if teachers became Special Constables they would then be empowered to control traffic outside the school. However, it was pointed out that if they became "Specials" they could be called upon for other duties as well. The suggestion was dropped.

One measure I took was to discontinue the ringing of the school bell – during the war it had been prohibited by law. I reasoned that if children were on the wrong side of the road when the bell stopped, they might panic and rush across just when they should be standing on the pavement. In the days of horses and carts, bell-ringing was perhaps justified, but times had changed with more and speedier forms of transport making the practice highly dangerous.

One day I was standing on the pavement waiting for the children to leave school, when I saw a policeman at the police station salute a man in civilian clothes who had ridden up on a motor cycle. It was only V.I.P.'s who were saluted and they usually arrived in cars. My curiosity was aroused so when all the children were safely across I strolled along to have a word with the constable who told me the man he had saluted was Captain Fairbairn, the Accident Officer to the Ministry of Transport. I walked into the station and told Captain Fairbairn that I needed his help to get the youngsters safely across the road. "Have you anything in mind?" he asked, so I suggested that if we had a "Zebra" pedestrian crossing outside the school I should not be acting illegally if, in holding up the traffic, I stood on the crossing. I also said that I thought it would be a good idea to have traffic lights at the cross roads to stop cars chasing through the village at speeds in excess of 40 m.p.h. He asked me to leave the matter in his hands, and about two months later he came into school and told me that he had got permission from the Ministry to install THREE pedestrian crossings in the High Street, but he could do nothing about the traffic lights as Rose Lane and Newark Lane were not major roads. I continued to see the children across the road for twelve years until school crossing patrols "Lollipop Men" were appointed.

Some years later the Ministry of Transport, I think it was, decided there were too many "Zebra" crossings up and down the country, and local authorities were instructed to remove as many as possible. The Guildford Rural District Council sent a panel to Ripley to discuss the matter with the Parish Council. I attended the meeting as an observer and told of the many attempts I had made to get the support of a variety of authorities to solve my problem, all of them unsuccessful. As it appeared that child safety on the roads was nobody's business, I had bypassed everybody and gone directly to the Ministry of Transport, which had authorised the crossings. The R.D.C. spokesman said that as we now had a Traffic Warden, a pedestrian crossing would be unnecessary. This proved to be a mistake, because owing to the building of the first stage of a new school on the opposite side of the road, children had to cross at times when the warden was off duty.

Having done what I could to secure a safe passage for the children I wondered if they could be helped to get home – all in one piece. I made a mental survey of Ripley and discovered several hazards for inexperienced and thoughtless children.

I thought that a film strip could be produced showing photographs of these danger spots, stressing both the incorrect and the correct behaviour while negotiating them. It would impress upon the children that these points were dangerous for pedestrians, would also train them to recognise other danger points and be valuable to them when later they drove cars and lorries themselves.

With the co-operation of the police a film strip was made of these areas and was used to warn children of these dangers. During the twenty-six years I was in Ripley several pedestrians were killed or injured on the main road, but there were no school children amongst them.

FAIR PLAY

Properly equipped children's playgrounds sited away from the traffic provide one way of keeping children off the roads. Despite the extensive area covered by Ripley Green, the village had no such playground until Mr. Richard Bondy came forward as the children's champion. Richard Bondy, who lived at Burnt Common, came to England as a refugee before the Second World War. He built up a very successful carpet business in Woking. Although he had none of his own, his fondness for children was well known and he was affectionately called "Uncle Dick". His interest in Ripley children continued long after the war and through his generosity organised trips were made to the seaside and the zoo.

In 1957 he supported a public collection to provide slides, swings and roundabouts for a Ripley playground and offered to match pound for pound the money received. Ripley British Legion organised the collection which amounted to about £200. Mr. Bondy more than doubled it!

Having raised the money to buy the equipment, a site for it had to be found. The Green was an obvious choice. On the west side is a deep circular depression about a hundred yards or more in diameter. It used to be the village pond but a deep sewer trench cut through the underground water supply which came from a spring in the garden of Rose Cottage in Rose Lane. When the sewers were laid, the water then followed the outside of the pipes and thus the pond remained drained. Children interested in botany spent many happy hours looking there for marsh specimens. When rain fell, water quickly gathered in the pond but drained away slowly, and even then the bottom remained very wet.

10. School Netball Team 1936/37
Mrs. Herrington
Peggy Hill, Joyce Milton, Winnie Farnfield, Hilda Hack,
Winnie Potter, Joyce Hatcher, Mary Morris

The members of the Playground Committee were of the opinion that the equipment should be placed round the rim. In this position it would be well away from the cricket green and it would take up relatively little space. The Parish Council approved, the Guildford R.D.C. approved, and all but one of the farren holders approved. Eventually we were given permission to install the apparatus, but it had to be located in the depression left by the pond. Then, when all work was complete, a period of heavy rain set in and turned the new playground back into a pond! It has long since dried out permanently.

Although there is no intentional connection with the previous paragraph, Ripley School was always noted for producing good swimmers. This is surprising considering the lack of facilities. Before the First World War, swimming in Surrey was not taken seriously and the children who attended urban schools where the local authorities provided facilities for children to be taught in enclosed and heated baths were most fortunate. After the war swimming was encouraged and in Surrey there were two competitions with trophies, one for schools using enclosed baths and one for schools using open water, i.e. rivers and lakes. Ripley was in the latter category, for they used the bathing place at Walsham Lock on the River Wey.

11. The bathing place Walsham Lock

The Woking schools were hardly better provided for, even though they used an open air swimming bath. The original bath is worth describing for it was supposed to be adequate for a town of twenty-five thousand people plus surrounding parishes. I do not remember the exact dimensions of the bath but it was approximately 100 ft. x 30 ft. It was dug on the site of a town rubbish dump, from which Woking Park ultimately evolved with its lido, hockey and cricket pitches.

It was seven feet deep at one end and three feet six inches at the other. The sides were boarded but the bottom was boarded only half way from the shallow end leaving the deep end with a bottom of yellow clay. I think there was a spring which slowly renewed the water in the bath, and there was no chlorination plant. The water was a deep rusty colour – quite opaque – and when one came from the bath there was a line of rusty scum across one's chin. I occasionally came across a dead frog or mouse whilst swimming in this soup. This rusty slime covered the boards on the bottom of the shallow end and they became so slippery that non-swimmers found it difficult to remain upright. I once saw two middle-aged men helping one another to learn the breast stroke; one of them slipped as he stood up and pulled on his companion who also slipped, and there they were half drowning each other in less than four feet of water.

Walsham Lock was even more dangerous. The bathing place was not the lock itself but about three hundred yards upstream. A bathing hut for the use of Ryde House School was set in an enclosure and kept locked. Everybody else undressed on the bank. The River Wey in its natural course meanders considerably, and bathing in this type of river can be extremely dangerous; in fact there were several drowning fatalities at what was known locally as "the bathing place".

Meandering rivers are sometimes linked up with a series of canals and cuttings to straighten the course for transport and drainage purposes. Locks have to be installed to maintain the level and here lies a hazard for the unwary. One Sunday, one of my pupils whose father had taken her on a fishing expedition to "The Anchor" at Pyrford fell into the lock as she was watching somebody opening one of the sluices. While onlookers were frantically searching for her, someone spotted a white bundle floating away downstream. It was the small girl who had gone through the sluice. She was soon rescued and resuscitated and was in school on Monday as lively as usual.

On another occasion Denis Hotson and Derek Holyoake, evacuees from Fulham and both about thirteen years old, went swimming on their own in the river Wey at Walsham. They both entered the water at the usual shallow place. Derek, who was a strong swimmer, made his way across to the opposite bank at the point where there was a deep hole. Denis, a weaker swimmer, attempted to follow but had only gone half-way across when he had to give up, and being out of his depth had to call for help. Derek dived back in and effected a classic rescue.

The rescue came to my notice so I reported it to the Royal Life Saving Association and Derek was awarded a certificate. It says much for our swimmers that, learning to swim under these difficult conditions, they still managed to win the Leon trophy in 1938.

WAR EFFORT
THE EVACUEES

In the summer of 1939, we were spending our summer holiday at Paignton, when a telegram recalled me to Ripley. On Sunday, September 3rd, war was declared on Germany, and the evacuation of children from our cities to the countryside began. Ripley Court School – Captain Pearce, staff and pupils – was evacuated to Wales. There Captain Pearce died and his body was returned to Ripley where he was buried in the family vault.

Ripley was chosen to receive children first from Fulham and then from Portsmouth. The school was used as a reception and medical inspection centre. Every child carried a bundle or case, and a square cardboard box containing a gas mask. A label with their name and address was attached to their clothes.

With two hundred and twenty children at school, our resources were strained to the utmost and eventually we had to overflow into the church hall, which was already in use for thirty difficult girls from Ryde House hostel. On certain afternoons the hall was used by church organisations and the children had to be accommodated in the main school building – three in a desk built for two.

One evening, at about 10.00 p.m. during the blackout, old Mr. Stanbridge, who lived in West End cottages, came to my door. He told me that he was having trouble with his three Fulham evacuee boys, aged 5,9 and 13. They had arrived in Ripley only the previous day and were billeted with him just off the main road. It seems that the Browning boys were homesick. Poor lads, I could sympathise with them. City life and village existence were so different, and running by their front door every twenty minutes was a Green Line coach which would transport them back to the streets of Hammersmith in one hour. Was it any wonder that they were dressed and lined up at their bedroom window, ready to climb out and catch the next coach home when Mr. Stanbridge looked in at them to say goodnight? I put on my hat and coat and walked across the allotments with the boys' aged foster parent. We all sat at a table, three boys, Mr. and Mrs. Stanbridge and myself. I told the boys that first thing tomorrow I would send a telegram to their father and ask him to come down as soon as he could, so long as they promised not to do anything silly like running away. Their father came down immediately and his visit sorted things out. The Browning boys settled down better than most of the evacuees and were among the last ones to leave the district for home.

Another evacuee family had a problem father in London. The two boys and a girl found shelter with my assistant gardener, Stephen Bradley and his wife, who lived in Newark Lane. Mrs. Bradley drew my attention to the state of the elder boy's boots. There was very little sole left and in one place on each foot, he was walking on his socks. The reception committee had by this time dispersed, so Mrs. Bradley had written to the father who was a clerk in the Ministry of Supply. She received no reply, so as the wet autumn was well advanced she came to me. The need was urgent so I telephoned the Secretary of the Guildford R.D.C. who said, "I can do nothing for a week, Mr. Dixon, as my Committee does not meet before then". I suggested that red tape should be cut and boots purchased at once. I told him that I would go to a local shoe shop, buy the boy a pair of boots and send the bill to the R.D.C. for presentation to the committee when next they met. He said, "Yes, do that Mr. Dixon, but pay for them and send me the receipted bill". Even in wartime, officialdom was so tied with red tape that there seemed no way of refunding the cost of the boots either from the father direct, or through some account. In order to reimburse me, a London County Council's Children's Christmas Party Fund was raided by a local organiser.

In almost every case the people of Ripley received the evacuated children with open arms, but the one exception was prevented from doing so by something which stood for religion. One Sunday, a number of evacuees arrived from Worthing. This evacuation was a sudden decision on the part of the Government because of the imminent possibility of invasion. Ripley was totally unprepared for it and the only available member of the reception committee was Mr. Tom Goodman, the Clerk to the Parish Council. It was obvious that he could not cope on his own so I contacted Mr. Brind, the Portsmouth evacuee teacher, and the two of us took over reception duties about 11.00 a.m. There was to be no church for us that day. We worked at registration throughout the day while Tom Goodman toured the area trying to find billets. When my wife and Mrs. Brind came out of church at 8.00.p.m. we only had to find places for one woman helper and her two grandchildren. We had gone through the village with a fine tooth-comb and then I suddenly remembered an elderly widower living alone in a four-bedroomed house. He had not been on our list because we could not have expected him to look after even one child, let alone a family. But this was a different proposition – a widow who would do everything for her two grandchildren in the accommodation provided. I personally called on him and presented our case. "No, Mr. Dixon", he said with a sob in his voice and tears in his eyes, "I am on good terms with them up there" – pointing heavenward – "and I do not wish to disturb the relationship". "But even Christians must eat and sleep on Sunday" I said and I quoted, "In as much as ye did it unto the least of these, ye did it unto me". "No, no, Mr. Dixon", he said "Not today. Come and see me tomorrow". "It will be too late then. Sleep well", I said as we parted. I never gave him a second chance as we managed to fit the evacuees in with a person who was needing a housekeeper. I was surprised that the Vicar adopted the same attitude. He said that it was wrong on the part of the authorities to evacuate the south coast on Sunday. I told him that as an ex-serviceman with the rank of Major, he would realise that nations at war do not recognise the Sabbath.

WAR EFFORT
OUR SHELTERS FROM THE STORMY BLAST

It was obvious to some people in the village that when war was declared bombs would drop on and around the village. We were only three and a half miles, as the bomber flies, from the Vickers aeroplane factory (now British Aerospace) at Weybridge. In fact the intensity of bombing at Ripley proved to be greater than that in Guildford or Woking.

Air raid shelters were being built for schools in the Cobham, Woking and Guildford areas, but the villages nearest Vickers received no such attention. Parents in Ripley were indignant and two or three leading villagers decided that if the authorities would not provide shelters for the children, they would.

I reported to the Chief Education Officer that the people in the village were determined to have shelters. The next day the Chief H.M.I., Mr. Heath, said "The idea is ridiculous. The Germans will not come over between the hours of nine and four, and somebody ought to tell the people so". I retorted that I would certainly not prophesy what the Germans would do. He said, "Well, would you come over in daylight?" and I replied that if I were in the German Air Force and were commanded to come, I would have to, whether I wanted to or not.

I then asked the County Architect if he would supply me with particulars relating to the Surrey County Council's requirements for the construction of shelters and he replied "No". I then asked him if he would view some block plans for approval if I submitted them to him. He replied "Yes". He only spoke those two words throughout the interview.

The block plans were produced by a member of a concrete construction company whose works were near the village, and I forwarded them to the County Architect. They were returned with his approval accompanied by a letter saying that the Surrey County Council would accept no liability or responsibility for them in any way.

The Vicar was quite opposed to the shelter scheme. Before we were allowed to put an excavator to work in the playground I had to sign a statement that I would reinstate the playground when the war was over. The Vicar urged me not to have anything to do with the project in case it affected my career. I had no doubt at all that what I intended to do was the right thing.

Concerts, whist drives, jumble sales, dances etc. now engaged our attention. As the money became available we bought pre-fabricated concrete sections. Cement, sand and labour were all given and machinery was loaned. Mr. Barrett, the portable building manufacturer on the Portsmouth Road, made a generous gift of seating for 200 children to use in the shelters. As yet we had no money for heating, lighting or ventilation. When completed, we had four shelters each capable of holding up to fifty children, and at one time we managed to pack a total of two hundred and fifty into them. They were amongst the best school shelters in Surrey.

When the shelters were almost completed, German planes bombed Vickers aircraft works at Weybridge in daylight and killed several workers who were just leaving the canteen. We had organised a garden fete on our tennis court at home for the shelter fund, and when the planes appeared almost overhead the tables and stalls were covered with white cloths and paper. The planes were very low and the black crosses were easily seen. It struck me that they would see our display of white cloths and look upon then as a sign of surrender. This would never do, so I hastily whipped them from the tables and stuffed then underneath.

The first intimation that they were enemy planes was when the anti-aircraft guns opened up on them. One bomber was brought down at Ockham and the wounded pilot was captured. He was brought to the doctor's surgery opposite the school for treatment but had to wait until Dr. Creet returned. The pilot had been wounded in the leg. Somebody managed to capture his flying boot complete with splinter holes and Fred Bushnell carried it around the village using it as a collecting box for our shelter fund.

The local A.R.P. group linked the school with the police station by means of a cable with a loud buzzer in Room 4. In this way we received immediate notice of all air-raid alerts. This room was later used for the Fire Watchers' nightly vigil in the centre of the village, and camp beds were installed for those resting.

All schools received a directive from County Hall that all windows in schools were to be faced on the inside with transparent material pasted to the glass to prevent shattering and consequent casualties if bombs dropped near. This order was repeated later, except that broad strips of brown gummed paper were to be fixed vertically and horizontally for the same purpose. Lucky were those heads of schools who had full-time male caretakers to put the order into effect. My part-time caretakers, both women, were unable to do it, and I had to carry out the work on my own.

One evening after school, two boys, John Hutson and a Portsmouth evacuee named Maurice Mercer, borrowed my wheelbarrow so that they could canvass their assigned area for salvage.Salvage thus collected was carted away, sorted, and used in the war effort. During the course of their perambulations the boys collected some glass soft drink bottles. They realised immediately that here was a grand opportunity to help themselves and the country at the same time by returning the bottles to a local shop at a penny or twopence a time. However duty called and they had to collect salvage, so they hurriedly hid the bottles in the hedge in Tom Gunner's garden which fronted Newark Lane.

I had been working on the allotments, but it was getting dusk as I walked home. I was barely indoors when the guns opened up, and this was followed a few moments later by a frantic banging on the knocker of our front door. I opened the door and John and Maurice nearly fell into my arms. "Can we come in, Mr. Dixon?" said John. "Jerry's up!" I brought them in and pushed Joan, my daughter, John and Maurice into the knee-hole of my desk. Then the bombs began to fall. The second one dropped on the edge of the Green about a hundred yards from our house and blew the large key out of the back door. "Coo!" said a voice, "That's the best we've had yet!" It was how Maurice would have voiced his appreciation of a firework display.

The third bomb demolished a house where the occupants had gone out; the fourth smashed the front of Tom Gunner's cottage, but the Gunners were in the back room and they and their dog were unhurt; the fifth dropped in the yard of Legge's tea shop (now Town and Country Cars) and only left a hole in the concrete; bomb six dropped fair and square on the cross-roads. The Vicar was at the door of the Vicarage speaking to John's sister Irene when they both heard it coming. They fell to the ground and the Vicar gallantly covered Irene's body with his own; another bomb fell on the tennis court at Chapel Farm in Rose Lane and the others just dropped in open fields. The plane's run was from north to south.

When the dust had settled John and Maurice sallied forth to "finish the job". They went to the spot where they had left their bottles – nothing but broken glass met their gaze. The bomb which smashed Tom Gunner's house had upset their plans to enter the money market! Tom Gunner and his wife collected all their unbroken china and glassware and placed it carefully in their shed which had not been damaged.

The next bombing of the village occurred later in the evening on a Saturday. On this occasion it was from east to west. Mr. Shoesmith's house was demolished (later rebuilt as Nos. 98 and 99 High Street) and he and his wife, daughter and mother-in-law were all buried in the rubble but were unhurt except for a slight cut on old Mrs. Carter's ear. On being rescued Mrs. Carter's chief concern was for her handbag which lay buried in the rubble! The second bomb dropped in an open space between a cluster of cottages on Greenside – the crater almost occupied the whole of the vacant area; the third bomb fell on Tom Gunner's shed containing all his salvaged glass and crockery and blew out the rear wall of a neighbouring cottage. A baker who had retired early for the night suddenly found himself still in bed at the bottom of a crater in the garden. The last bomb dropped on the allotments.

The following day – Sunday – Mr. Chapman, a local butcher, and his friend Richard Bondy visited me after lunch. Mr. Bondy did the talking: "Mr. Dixon, I have a proposition to make to you. I will pay to ventilate, heat and light your shelters with electricity on one condition – that you allow the village people to use them out of school hours". This seemed too good to be true. Of course, there never had been any intention to exclude the adults from the shelters for they had provided the money for them and all the labour.

Some nights later, in the early hours of the morning, some 1500 incendiary bombs fell on and around the village. Fortunately little damage was done but the scenic effect was beautiful. Trees and hedges were silhouetted in black against a background of white light and it was as if one had been transported to fairyland.

Many families evacuated from the Elephant and Castle area in London used the shelters, and when London was bombed the shelters were placed at the disposal of the people who had lost their homes. These unfortunate people were accommodated in the church hall; the women slept on the stage with drawn curtains, and the men slept on the fixed seats along the sides or on the floor. I went down two or three times and on the last occasion I took some old safety razors, blades and shaving soap which were in short supply, for the people had brought nothing with them. As I entered the hall an old lady said "Cor lumme Guv'nor, don't bring us anything more or you'll make us cry". We spent a total of seventy-six hours in the shelters – forty-two for ordinary daylight raids and thirty-four for the flying bombs or "doodle-bugs",, later known as V1's to distinguish them from the V2's which were rockets. These two weapons were calculated by Hitler to devastate southern England.

One day at about 11.00 a.m. a V1 was heard approaching the village followed by an explosion. The children were in the shelters but from my position in the playground I could see a plume of smoke rising and it was clear that it had fallen on Ripley Green.

It occurred to me that the children would be worried about the safety of their parents, so I went first to the Infants' shelter. I need not have worried. As I descended the steps I heard the strains of "Jesus loves me this I know" coming from fifty childish throats. This was undoubtedly Miss Marsh's contribution to their morale. In the second shelter the children were completely calm and unruffled, and as I reached it I heard "Pack up your troubles in your old kit bag". How often had I heard that sung during the shelling in the First World War and at the time I never imagined that I would hear English boys and girls singing it under similar circumstances. In the last shelter where the eldest children were, I heard the refrain ".....Put that pistol down, babe, put that pistol down. Pistol packing Momma, put that pistol down". This popular war-time song evidently indicated what they thought about the war.

I was so impressed by the behaviour of the 5 – 11 year old children that I thought the parents should know and appreciate the work of the teachers who were mainly responsible for them, so I sent a few special lines to the Vicar for inclusion in the parish magazine.

While the children were in the shelters the time was never wasted and the opportunity was taken to commit to memory prose and verse passages and multiplication tables.

One night a very funny incident occurred in the ranks of the Home Guard at an observation post in Polesden Lane which had been constructed in a tree. During an alert, when German bombers were in the vicinity, the post was manned by one sentry, with a corporal and two men on the ground. Major Kay was on his rounds and when he arrived at the post there was a battle royal going on between the group on the ground and the sentry up the tree. Major Kay enquired the reason for this strange behaviour in the presence of the enemy and the two accounts went along these lines. The corporal said "Well sir, we was standing 'ere at the foot of the tree when suddenly old 'Aynes (the sentry) up there started buzzing things down at us, so we retaliated". Haynes' version was exactly opposite to this. He said "I was up the tree, sir, and them blighters started chucking things up at me". The truth was that the ack-ack guns were firing at the planes and the splinters were falling round the group on the ground. They thought that old Haynes had suddenly gone mad and quickly reacted in the way he had described, much to his annoyance.

Mr. Heath, the H.M.I., was visiting us when an alert came through the buzzer system. I wondered if he remembered telling me that the Germans would never come over between the hours of 9 a.m. and 4 p.m. Actually he was quite right, they sent their pilotless planes to bombard us instead! The warnings came as soon as they were reported flying towards the coast where some of them were shot down. They quickly covered the forty miles to Ripley. They were extremely noisy and when they passed overhead sounded like loose ironmongery.

By this time we were adept at getting into the shelters. When an alert came through, the classes were taken out to their respective shelters but instead of filing into them they remained on the surface. Blackboards and easels were erected and lessons carried on in daylight and fresh air. Each class divided into two and when the clanking machinery was heard a whistle was blown and, at the word "DIVE", each group entered the shelter at a different entrance and the whole school would be underground in ten seconds.

At the conclusion of the war, I submitted a report to every parent and to all helpers in the erection of the shelters, including all known donors. I said that one thing for which the war was fought was that there should be freedom from fear. Through the shelters this had been achieved for the children and their parents at a cost of sixpence (2½p) per child hour. From the financial point of view alone it was well worth it, but the value to village morale was incalculable. This can be proved by comparison with the village of Send which had no school shelters. A V1 fell on some cottages at Burnt Common. Mr. Gay, the headmaster of St. Bede's Secondary School, closed his school at once and sent the children to their homes, including those who lived at Burnt Common. The head teacher of the Primary School followed suit. No child at Ripley School had relatives who were amongst the casualties, but two of the children lived in one of the nearby houses. The Governors and Managers of the two Send schools communicated with County Hall demanding shelters before they considered it safe to open the schools again. They were provided with open trenches as a substitute. This of course took time, and during that time our school remained open and attendance remained steady around the 90% mark.

At the conclusion of the war I received a visit from the Chief County Inspector, Mr. Gunton. As he was leaving the school I drew his attention to the shelters and asked him if he knew their history. He told me that he had heard something about them, then turning to me he said "I think they are a monument to you, Mr. Dixon". I then told him about the piece of paper containing my signature and held by the Vicar, where I promised to reinstate the playground at the conclusion of hostilities. He immediately "blew up" and said that he had never come across such an instance where a person's sense of social service had been treated in such a shabby manner. He went back to Kingston, gave them a piece of his mind and I received a letter from the Chief Education Officer to the effect that the Surrey County Council had accepted responsibility for the shelters. (N.B. The shelters were among the last remaining in the county, fitting reminders of the war, until the school itself was demolished in 1982).

SCHOOL DINNERS
(MAKING A MEAL OF IT...)

When I commenced my duties at Ripley in January 1936, I found that there were many children remaining at school during the dinner hour. They lived too far away to return home for a midday meal. Most of these children travelled distances of up to 2½ miles to school in all weathers and often arrived with stockings, boots and clothes soaking wet. The clothes then had to be hung over radiators, fire-guards and the backs of chairs to dry out. For some children I managed to get an issue of bus tickets but they were the exceptions. A teacher was paid sixpence (2½p) a day to look after the children during the midday break and this was a very useful and welcome addition to a small salary.

One day I stayed rather later at school before going home to lunch, and I saw the children walking about the playground eating their lunches from paper bags. There were no seats and no play-sheds in the grounds, and I felt quite guilty about going home to a nice hot meal served in comfort. I therefore requisitioned unbreakable plates and beakers and a quantity of American cloth [1] which was cut up into sizes for covering the tops of the desks. I then wrote to John Strudwick, a County Councillor, who was also the Hon. Secretary of the Surrey Teachers' Association, deploring the lack of catering facilities in rural schools.

Some days later I received a letter with the envelope embossed "HOUSE OF COMMONS". It was a request by James Chuter Ede for a report on the catering facilities at Ripley School, together with any suggestions which I cared to make. In my report I described what I had seen when the children had placed their "dinners" on their plates: some had one or two pennyworth of broken biscuits or potato crisps, some had two slices of bread and butter and sugar, while others had bread and butter with an apple or orange.

Between the Wars the Managers could start a school canteen with a loan from the Local Education Authority. This, of course, was possible in large elementary schools, grammar schools and technical schools, but not in small rural schools where parents' wages were very low (at this time a farm worker for example was paid the weekly wage of about 30/- (£1.50)). Such canteens could never pay their way, let alone repay the loan. My report drew Mr. Ede's attention to this and suggested that the loan should be replaced by a grant, for here was a clear case for subsidised meals. To my surprise I received a congratulatory paragraph in the "Surrey Teacher", and later I learned that the report had been of assistance in supporting Mr. Ede's efforts to inaugurate school meals throughout the country.

After the War commenced on 3rd September 1939, and food rationing was subsequently introduced, it was inevitable that school meals would become the order of the day. Classroom 4 was adapted as a kitchen, and a cook and kitchen staff were appointed. The teachers and I willingly undertook the additional chores and the consequent reduction of our free time. It was not incumbent on me to take a share in supervising the meals but, as it was a voluntary effort on the part of the teachers, I would not ask them to do something which I was not prepared to do myself. It was part of our combined war effort to provide the children with additional food and allow the mothers to engage in work of national importance.

After the War, however, I found that parents were taking advantage of these facilities during the midday break. I was annoyed that my staff had become child minders. It was similar to ordering a doctor in a hospital to assist with serving meals to the patients. Teachers were supervising the activities of children living only one hundred yards from school whose mothers were not employed outside the home and whose family income was adequate to provide a good midday meal at home.

We used to have a little trouble over children's likes and dislikes regarding the food they were given. I overcame this by sending a circular letter to the parents, or giving them a copy on admission of a new child, telling them that as they paid for a dinner for their child, it was for me to see that the child had value for money and that there would be little waste. If on the other hand the mother did not wish her child to have certain types of food, a note would be made of the fact and these items would not be put on the child's plate. Henceforth I should need a written and signed request for such alterations to be made to the standard menu. This worked very well but it led, in one case, to an amusing request written by the boy himself:-

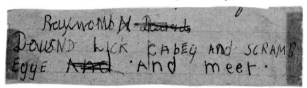

Interpreted, this reads Raymond Deards doesn't like cabbage and scrambled egg and meat!

(1) American cloth was an enamelled oilcloth used for table covering before the arrival of plastic surfaced cloths.

PEOPLE OF THE VILLAGE

I have described the village, its development, its history, its buildings, some of its leading characters and, in some detail, its school, but I have said very little about the people without whom there would be no village.

People who do not live in the countryside are sometimes deceived by that slow, drawling speech and the air of submission in the countryman. These are a product of both his struggle against, and co-operation with, the forces of nature. As a result of his environment, the countryman is fiercely independent. He is naturally patient because nature works slowly and he would not have it otherwise, because when nature works quickly, then comes disaster.

The countryman is also religious. I do not mean that he necessarily attends church regularly; in fact he may only appear at Harvest Festivals. When it is time for church he may be attending to his animals, or working in his own garden, or resting at home, after a week of toiling against the stubborn soil and weeds. However, the fact that he sows his grain, shows that he recognises the existence of a power which he cannot understand; he may not say as much, but obviously he is a firm believer in miracles.

The farm worker, apart from being in good health, must have a good head on his shoulders. He has to be a vet, an engineer, even something of a scientist in branches relating to soil, plant life and weather lore, and for all this he is one of the worst paid members of the community. I have mentioned my old caretaker, Mr. Gunner. He once told me how he and his brother Tom used to "shoot" pigeons at the request of a farmer. The pigeons were a pest at harvest time and used to fly from the woods on Hungry Hill, settle on the stooked corn and feed until they could hardly take off again. This meant a big loss to the farmer, so he engaged Bill and Tom Gunner to thin out the pigeons a little. Their payment was on a per capita basis, which of course covered the cost of cartridges. The two brothers each took a part of the field, and there dug a hole in the ground. Round the hole they stooked the sheaves in groups of about ten or twelve, made themselves comfortable in the hole and waited for the birds to come. Then all they had to do was to seize the birds as they came to feed and without any fuss despatch them. In this way, the birds were not frightened from the field because no gun was fired, and there was a plentiful supply of pigeons for sale. I wonder if a townsman could have thought of that?

Mr. Gunner also told me how his 'old Dad' rarely went to the chemist but found remedies for their childhood complaints in the fields and hedgerows. One such remedy struck me as being most uncommon. He used to go out on the Green and catch an adder. He would then extract the fat which lies at the base of the skull on each side of the spine. This fat, he would render down and make on ointment which was used on their "cuts and boils".

The mention of chemists reminds me of the only one in Ripley. Soon after moving to the village I needed a prescription. The chemist's shop had a Dickensian atmosphere about it and behind the counter was a character who could also have come from a Dickens novel. He was an odd little man, unkempt and with a permanent grin on his face. He wore a rag of a soft collar, a red tattered tie pulled round to one side under his ear, and a week's growth of beard. He asked me my business and I told him I had a prescription to be made up and would he please ask Mr. Allenby when I could call for it. He said, "I will make it up for you, sir, and it will be ready in twenty minutes". Thinking that I had misheard I said "Will Mr. Allenby be able to prepare it so soon?" He replied, "I will do it right away sir". I did not like the look of things at all. I went outside and heaved a sigh of relief as I espied the reassuring figure of the police sergeant – Sergeant Bright. I told him what I was thinking, and asked him if it was safe in the little man's hands. He laughed and said "Oh that's old Harry. He's all right. I've never known him make a mistake yet". Still feeling some misgivings, I made further enquiries and it turned out that "Old Harry" was a clever man. He was the qualified chemist and his brother, who was the owner of the shop, was unqualified. It appeared that Harry had had a breakdown consequent upon his studies but it had not impaired his ability as a chemist. I have also heard him speaking in German and French to customers. It was an unusual shop in other ways, since one could also buy eggs, dog biscuits and garden seeds there. I believe also that, at one time, teeth were extracted! When the Allenbys died, the shop came into the possession of Kenneth White. That was in December 1943 and I was glad to see that one of my ex-pupils, John Hutson, was promptly employed. Here was a sudden jump from the early 19th century to the mid-20th century. Ken White was an energetic business man but with a simple desire to contribute to the community. In a few weeks the place was turned upside-down and a modern dispensary was installed. In these changes John Hutson played his part. The late Dr. Ralli Creet then challenged White to produce Penicillin Filtrate, a rare and new medication reserved almost exclusively for HM Forces at the time of D-day. The drug was soon produced and after standardisation by the late Dr. Madson at the Royal Surrey Hospital in Guildford, the pharmacy was licensed by the Ministry of Health to manufacture and supply to hospitals, etc.

There were two bakers in the village – Weller, at what is now Hartley Antiques, and Maurice Collins on the corner of Rose Lane who also sold garden seeds, dog biscuits, eggs and scent. On Christmas Day, anyone passing at about 12.45 p.m. would have seen a group of people assembled at the side of the baker's shop by the passage-way leading to his ovens. These people would have come with perambulators, wheelbarrows, hand-carts and even by motor car. They would all be waiting for the opening of the oven doors whence would emerge the appetizing smell of cooked turkeys, chickens, ducks, etc. These were

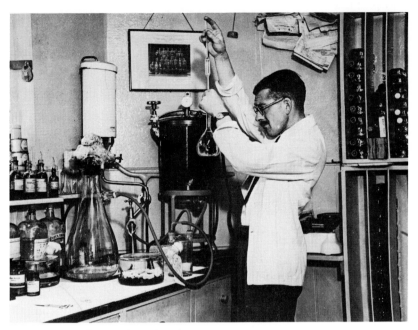

12. Ken White in his pharmacy

13. John Hutson, the chemist's assistant c.1945

all placed in the oven when the bread was taken out and emerged just in time to be placed on the dinner table.

On the opposite side of the road was the village forge, a never failing source of interest to the youngsters who revelled in the entertainment supplied. The smouldering fire, suddenly bursting into life like a miniature volcano at a few pumps of the bellows, the sparks flying like fireworks as the heavy hammer hit the red hot metal to shape it to fit the horse's hoof, the pungent smell of burnt hoof and the wonder of paring and nailing into the hoof without hurting the animal; the excitement when a horse was restive and finally the animal itself which could be a huge Shire or a Shetland pony, or an in-between, carriage horse, hunter or cob – they were all objects of interest and affection.

Then there was the blacksmith himself, old Bill Heath, who was a Parish Councillor, and continually on the alert for any infringements of the rights of the villagers. Sir Oliver Simmonds, who was then the owner of Dunsborough House, had dared to put a padlock on a gate to a right of way. There was a stile there but prams and carts needed to use the gateway. Bill took a cold chisel and hammer and soon dealt with that.

I have previously referred to the independent character of the countryman. If one helps them in some way it is appreciated and repaid in full as the following stories show.

I discovered that my caretaker, Bill Gunner, was burning midnight oil at school one night a week, so I asked him about it. "It's because of the Red Cross meeting" he said, "Every Thursday night they comes and it's well after ten when they finishes". I asked him if he was paid for the extra work and was told that he received nothing. I knew that the County Council were paying for the light and coal used and I felt that advantage was being taken of my caretaker. The Hon. Secretary of the Red Cross group was employed in the County Architect's Department and he knew the rules governing school lettings. He told me that the Captain had said that the group could hold meetings there without charge. He also agreed that Mr. Gunner should be remunerated for his extra work. At the conclusion of the session he passed the hat round for Mr. Gunner and collected £2.10s.0d. (£2.50p) which was the equivalent of two and a half weeks wages. One evening the following summer, my caretaker came to my house bearing a large dish of raspberries from his allotment and said, "Thank you for getting that money for us las' winter, zur".

One April during the war, a man arrived at my house on his bicycle. He explained that he had cycled from Send because a friend of his suggested that he should come and see me as he had a problem. It was indeed a problem. Being illiterate, he wanted me to complete his application for a State Pension but he had been a foundling. At length we got things sorted out and he put his "X" which I witnessed. Then he stood up, put his hand in his pocket and said, "Well sir, how much is that?" "I can do it for a friend, I suppose", I replied. "Well", he said, "I never forgets my promises and I'll see as you 'as a duck for your Christmas dinner". On Christmas Eve, my friend came again on his bicycle carrying a basket which he handed to me, saying, "For your Christmas dinner, sir". Inside was a duck, plucked and ready for the oven.

THE END OF THE FURROW

Only those who have experienced the ending of their life's work and the beginning of retirement can fully enter into my feelings on that day in 1961 which was to be my last day at school. For my predecessor, Mr. Blaxland, the emotional strain had been more the he could stand. He had remained cheerful when he had once received ninety-two bee stings, but his last leave-taking caused him to break down. Each of us had spent almost twenty-six years at the helm. I steeled myself for the approaching ordeal which was to be in the Church Hall in the evening. I had told the Vicar that I claimed the right of an old soldier to "simply fade away" but, although he was new to the village, the Reverend George Street was not going to let me have such an inglorious end.

When I was about to leave school that afternoon, the door opened and in walked the Vicar, his wife and a group of young mothers whom I recognised as some of my "old girls". The Vicar explained that the group wanted to make a separate presentation to mark the occasion. When they were seated in the well-known desks, one of my ex-pupils came forward and presented me with a travelling alarm clock in a red case. It was inscribed "F. DIXON, From OLD SCHOLARS OF RIPLEY SCHOOL". I was quite unprepared for this and I am afraid that my thanks were halting and punctuated by gulps. As they were leaving, a five year old pupil at school lifted up her face to be kissed and her seven year old sister put her arms around my neck and also kissed me. Then one of the parents said "Aren't you going to treat us all alike?" – and so I did!

At the entrance to the Church Hall that night, I was met by one of the Italian boys in school. He was aged eleven and only a few days beforehand I had had to make him 'touch his toes' not only for truanting, but at the same time playing by the river in Wellingtons which could have drowned him had he fallen in. He was carrying a bottle of Coca Cola complete with straw and he said, "For you Mr. Dixon". Inside the hall, I found many old friends assembled and it proved most difficult to drink 'Coke', shake hands and talk simultaneously.

Arriving at the platform I found representatives of Managers, ex-pupils, friends and staff. Peter Conisbee, who chaired the proceedings, had been one of my gardening class boys and in his remarks he referred to the event. I was very touched by the fact that he had organised a public subscription and had returned from holiday specially to chair the meeting and make the presentation. This consisted of a garden lounger and a cheque. Mr. Cartwright, a Churchwarden, presented me with a cheque from the Church, and Arnold Porter, a member of the staff, gave my wife one of the largest boxes of chocolates I have ever seen. Later, the Managers visited me at home and gave me a stainless steel spade.

There is now another and younger hand on the plough and I have no doubt at all that he has chosen as his mark the one which I chose more than a quarter of a century before. He has quite literally entered a fairer field. There is a new building erected on a site of more than two acres, which includes a playing field and playground. There is a spacious, light, airy and warm hall, a headmaster's room, a secretary's room, a medical inspection room and a staff-room furnished with upholstered chairs and decorative curtaining. The large boiler is oil-fired and there is a full-time caretaker. A well-equipped kitchen serves meals in the adjoining hall and NOT IN A CLASSROOM. The heated toilets are in the main block and in due course there will be a swimming pool.

I have prepared this record because I think that my time at Ripley marked the end of an era and the beginning of a new and better one for the children of the village. I am envious of my successor's good fortune, but I would not have it otherwise, for my satisfaction derives from the fact that at long last the children are taught under conditions worthy of them.